SELF-MANAGEMENT BY INTROSPECTION

(A POWERFUL PROCESS FOR EMPOWERING YOUR PERSONALITY AND CAREER)

A PRAGMATIC APPROACH
FOR
STEERING YOUR DESTINY

A COMPREHENSIVE SELF-ADDRESSED BOOK
TO KNOW YOURSELF
FOR
BECOMING REAL ACHIEVER AND LEADER
IN YOUR PROFESSIONAL CAREER

By

R M ONKAR

(Lt. Col. Retd.)

SELF-MANAGEMENT BY INTROSPECTION

A POWERFUL PROCESS
FOR
EMPOWERING YOUR PERSONALITY AND CAREER

A PRAGMATIC APPROACH
FOR
STEERING YOUR DESTINY

By

R M ONKAR

(Lt. Col. Retd.)
B.E. (Hons), M.E. , F.I.E.T.E.
Advisor, Career Management & Art of Living (FENG SHUI)
Ex. Jt. Managing Director
Punjab Communications Limited, Mohali (Punjab)

AUTHORSPRESS

Worldwide Circulation through Authorspress Global Network
First Published 2010
by
Authorspress
E-35/103, Jawahar Park
Laxmi Nagar, Delhi-110 092
e-mail: authorspress@yahoo.com

Self-management by introspection
ISBN 978-81-7273-498-5

Printed in India at Tarun Offset, Delhi.

Dedicated to the memory
of my grandfather
Late

Shri Laxmanrao Ramji Onkar

who inspired and encouraged
me during my childhood to have
vision, ambition and will-power
for my bright future.

Prologue

At the outset, I wish to clarify that what have been stated in the title of this book covers a broad spectrum of the objective, pertaining to Self-management. And the basic process for its effective achievement is introspection which is a self-addressed, self-centric and self-practised exercise performed by one exclusively on oneself. As a result, the subject of the book is apparently covered in two distinct parts, the first part dealing with the process of introspection which eventually leads to self-assessment, self-appraisal for career selection and self development. The second part covers its practical applications which primarily include development of one's personality, preparation for facing personal interviews, management of service career for promotions and advancement, interconnectedness of destiny, self-awakening for enlightenment and finally becoming an achiever against heavy odds and adverse conditions. Thus, the process of introspection plays a very significant role in discovering one's positive and negative qualities, strengths and weaknesses, aptitude and interest areas. Consequently, it leads to empower one's service career. As a result, self-management becomes a broad-based multidimensional activity and eventually emphasizes the basic principle of commencing performance of one's activities from yourself. In other word, it beckons one to remain at the centre-stage of one's all lifetime activities.

As regards understanding the scope of self-management, it covers various facets and aspects of one's life such as stated below:

a) Personality development and career advancement.

b) Healthy career growth with timely promotions.

c) Achievement of self-confidence in facing competitive personal Interviews.
d) Establishing personal identity and its effective projection.
e) Exploitation of one's full inherent and hidden power and potential.
f) Application of cure and remedies for career illness, derailment and failure whenever they occur.
g) Self–appraisal for launching self-employment schemes/ services/enterprises.
h) Unfolding secrets of one's destiny and timely application of course correction to its path.
i) Understanding relationship of one's karmas with one's brain-mind combined operation.

Since everyone is interested to know and achieve them in their life, it is imperative that one should know the technique for achievement. The mere statement and advice that one should do introspection is a casual approach and it is not sufficient and meaningful for producing the desired result. So, one should now go ahead to comprehensively find out in this book the technique of introspection and its significance, relevance and rationality in organising self-management of one's career.

Special Features of the Book

1. A self-addressed, self-centric and self-practised technique for discovering one's inner self.
2. Offers effective guidance to clear the confused state of one's mind about selection of proper, productive and meaningful career.
3. Appraises one about the hidden treasure of one's strong and weak points and emphasizes need for enhancing and exploiting one's strong points and controlling your weak points.
4. Enables one to effectively adopt a roadmap for self-development and achieve career advancement as well as personality development.
5. Offers comprehensive guidance for preparing and facing interviews and in-house selection boards.
6. Opens a golden gate for one to effectively manage, Divdersify and enrich one's career.
7. Offers the key to reveal the secret of one's success or failure or good or bad luck.
8. Awakens one from slumber of ignorance to knowledge, wisdom and enlightenment about one's self.
9. Finally, enables one to realistically look into one's destiny and reveals the key role played by one's mind in structuring and operationalising one's personal qualities.

This Book

- Is reader friendly and offers comprehensive guidance, advice and counseling to a wide spectrum of the readers on their service career related issues and prospects.
- Makes them self-confident, self-reliant and enterprising to face risks and challenges in life.
- Has well structured text with its thoughtful and pragmatic presentation.

So, don't miss and remain without it.

Acknowledgements

Firstly, I express my deep gratitude to Prof. Dr. M. L. Madan, former Vice Chancellor of Dr. Punjabrao Deshmukh Agricultural University, Akola (M.S.) for going through the original manuscript. He emphasized the importance and benefits of the subject for careers of the readers of a very wide spectrum and pointed out Career Advancement as the focal theme of my book. Later, he advocated students in his lectures and addresses that they should often do introspection and self-assessment.

Dr. D. A. Deshpande is another person to whom I owe my sincere gratitude because he encouraged me to write a book on this career-oriented subject of intimate concern to our youth. He also meticulously went through my original script, made many corrections and gave valuable suggestions that encouraged me to delve deeper into the multidimensional aspects of the subject matter.

I cannot deny the valuable contributions made by other learned and high ranking persons like Dr. R.T. Gahukar, Dr. K. S. Yawalkar, Shri, C. S. Kirpekar and Shri M. W. Onkar who carefully went through my original script and brought out the immense utility of the subject matter. They highlighted in their remarks the importance of the subject and its usefulness to college students for career selection career, to the parents for guiding their wards, to the businessmen for starting enterprise / industry, trade or self-employment, to the employees in the industrial units and organisations / institutions for managing their careers and to the employers for promoting their employees for senior and higher positions of responsibilities. Their forethoughts and wide ranging remarks about my book are pragmatic, rational and classical. I am deeply grateful to them for their thoughtful assessment and judgement about my book. I also thank Shri Ravindra Karandikar for going through the final manuscript of this book and making appropriate corrections and modifications wherever needed.

Finally, I am grateful to Sudarshan Kcherry, Managing Director of Authorspress, for publication of my book.

R M Onkar

Personal Letter from the Author to the Readers about this Book

Dear Readers,

I am aware that some of you might feel hesitant and doubtful and think why you should purchase this book and how much beneficial and helpful it would prove to your career prospects and advancement, considering the money you have to spend on its purchase.

Having myself gone through various stages of career related problems and advancement under different service and environmental conditions, I propose to share my ideas, experience, viewpoints and vision with you and really show the positive way as to how you should proceed on your career road map and face eventual roadblocks en route to your destination.

Some of you may feel that they will cross the bridge when they come across it. Some of you may believe in their destiny and leave career problems and related issues to it. Some of you may not feel the necessity of knowing much about your career as you may perhaps feel confident to achieve progressive success in your careers and some of you may not bother to know about your weak points and wish to proceed on the basis of the gut feelings.

Introspection is the issue as well as the subject which is much talked about and referred to. It is too often emphasized and forcefully advocated for us to practice and pursue. Unfortunately, nobody says how it should be done or shows the practical way of doing it. Hence, the word introspection remains a myth, uncared, ignored and the least followed and understood.

I have tried to bridge this gap by giving and describing a Direct Personal Method with the comprehensive list of positive and negative qualities for marking their presence and levels within your-Self. The title of book itself and its theme are clear in their objectives and purpose. Besides, the special features of the book are given on its back cover page and each chapter is preceded with a set of questions for the sake of easy and clear understanding of the subject matter of the concerned chapter.

Issues of Introspection, Self-Assessment, Self-Appraisal, Self-Development and Self-Interrogation which are treated as five pillars of your real positive Personality Development are very important and relevant in today's highly competitive career oriented environment and global market of the 21st Century. You have to learn how to successfully manage your career and seek its advancement. In fact, you need positive guidance at every stage of your career for effectively managing your career and achieving success.

In this respect, this book offers you comprehensive guidance and advice for successfully managing your career with prospect for achieving senior and high level promotions and appointments. You come to know the technique for effective Self Development that makes you Self-Confident, Self-Reliant and finally Enterprising to face the Risks and Challenges of the life. You are able to distinguish between success and failure and delink them from the mystic aspect of your Destiny. At the same time, you are acquainted with the multi-dimensional aspects of Introspection that plays positive role in enrichment and enlightenment of your life.

You will observe that this book is remarkably Reader Friendly and Reader Interactive thereby generating one-to- one dialog with you. At every stage, you remain at the center stage of your lifetime activities and performance. That eventually makes you the Architect of your own Destiny.

I am quite certain that you, belonging to one of the user categories as given in the list attached to this letter will immensely benefit by reading this book and will definitely make all the difference to your performance, personality and career. So, don't miss Valuable Self-Driven Guide to steer your Personality and Career to higher levels of glory and Prosperity.

Nagpur 440006

R. M. Onkar
(Lt. Col. Retd.)

Comprehensive List of the Users and Beneficeries Belonging to a Wide Spectrum of Categories

The book is intended to serve the interests of students and candidates WHO

1. Have passed graduation and wish to appear for competitive examinations at state and national levels.
2. Wish to launch their careers in service, business or industry or become small scale entrepreneurs or undertake self-employment.
3. Wish to appear for interviews or service selection boards for selection.
4. Are awaiting placement and are about to start careers in service.
5. Are already in service and wish to manage their careers for achieving promotions during their service periods.
6. Wish to successfully manage their careers and rise in ranks and status in order to reach higher or top positions through successive promotions.
7. Wish to gain insight into their behaviour, nature and personality traits for effective development and excelling in a highly competitive environment.
8. Wish to adopt a Self-Development program for enriching their careers and improving promotional prospects.
9. Wish to control and exercise restraint on their important negative qualities which are likely to cause setbacks in their careers.
10. Wish to boldly face risks and challenges to rise in their enterprising careers.
11. Wish to become an Achiever and Leader in their life against heavy odds and adversities.
12. Wish to discover the secrets of their career oriented Destiny.

Preface

After my retirement from service of over 35 years, consisting of 22 years in the Army and the rest in a reputed State Public Sector Undertaking initially at senior ranks and later at nearly the top position of its management, I could look back and recollect my fairly long service period. It mainly included my participation in two Indo-Pak Wars, once working at the planning level in the Army Headquarters and then at the active field level on the battlefront while serving in the Army. Despite my basically rural and agricultural background associated with the normal shortcomings and drawbacks, I could achieve specialisation in the engineering field of telecommunication and later in the marketing field, and contribute substantially to both organisations of the Army and Industry. I frankly admit that they in fact rewarded me with promotions at senior and high level ranks and appointments of high responsibilities and accountability during my entire fairly long service period.

During my service tenures as well as thereafter, I had opportunities and occasions to travel widely within and outside our country. During one of my long stays in Singapore, I could extensively read and study the Chinese Art of Living called FENG SHUI. The essence of FENG SHUI is to know yourself first so that you can arrange balancing of your personal energy pattern with that of your surroundings (home and office) in order to accomplish harmony which eventually leads to achieve peace, happiness and prosperity in life. Being aware about our Indian astrology, my attention was drawn in both cases to the cosmic forces of the Heaven and Earth which are determined by the orbital movements of the planets. It is believed that your energy pattern is determined at the time of birth in the presence of then existing cosmic forces including gravitational field of the earth present at the birthplace. It is then carried with you throughout your life as an imprint of your destiny.

During the course of my meetings with students of 10 + 2 classes and graduate levels and while advising on career and courses, I asked a number of them to write at least five good points and five bad or weak points about them. It was surprising to find that none could do, nor came forward partially, nor volunteered to know how to do it. They simply answered that they didn't know. I was indeed baffled and surprised to see this pathetic attitude towards their Self. The question did then arise in my mind as to how and on what basis I should render advice and guide them if they did not know their strong and weak points, potential, abilities, aptitude and interest areas.

I talked to a number of students of Engineering and Commerce and asked about their objective for doing the course and about their future plans. I also appraised them about the bright service prospects and careers in Defence services and Para Military forces at officer's level where a large demand exists today. I could not get any precise idea about their objectives and future plans and in some cases, it was found limited to a very low level-objective of getting some immediately available employment. Besides, the candidates who were selected for employment were not aware about the professional skills and techniques, required for successfully managing their careers, and they were mostly found to believe in the destiny for their success or failure in future.

I have stated this extensive background and personal experience which have indeed prompted and motivated me to write this book on the basic theme of Knowing Thyself directly which does not need any reference to astrologers and palmists. I could intently and deeply dwell on the subject of Destiny and its important role in your service career. I was keen to know the real cause of human success and failure in this life. I also wanted to analyse why some persons reach higher steps of the promotion ladder while some lag behind or stagnate at low or middle levels in many organisations and industries. I also observed that the candidates who appeared for interviews were not aware about expectations of their employers nor did they enquire about their viability and market position.

The background, as explained above, led me to think that it was the right and appropriate time for me to take up the issue of immediate concern to our youth who are invariably found struggling to get proper career guidance and advice about placement, promotion and finally advancement during their service periods. Therefore I strongly felt that they should first draw their attention to themselves and do introspection and self-assessment honestly, sincerely and truthfully, and then decide the course of direction and action for achieving their lifetime objectives.

I came across a number of books on subjects of career guidance and personality development. But none of them was found to have pointedly addressed this issue of Knowing Thyself with sincere efforts for carrying out introspection, self- assessment and self-appraisal. No efforts have been made to correlate them with one's success or failure for actually determining one's destiny. I propose to bridge this gap in understanding and advocate our youth to deeply look to themselves and discover their strong and weak or positive and negative points, and inner hidden treasure of potential in order to drive and motivate them to achieve their lifetime objectives of materialistic and spiritual nature, such as fortune, wealth, fame, prosperity and, finally, happiness and peace of mind..

With this objective in my mind that should extend meaningful benefits to the youth in the positive manner, I have structured the entire subject of this book and projected it in nine chapters with proper introduction and concluding remarks. The special features of the book are highlighted on its backcover for giving you its essence and perspective at a glance.

Here, I have given an Annexure 4 to Chapter 6 which describes the technique for writing one's own Personal Confidential Report on one's performance under various heads, thereby giving enough information about one's capabilities and potentialities with provision for adopting remedial measures for self-improvement and enrichment of one's life. I have also thought of those who come across failure especially at the threshold of their career, and hence enclosed an Annexure 3 to Chapter 4 as a consoling note for them. In chapters 6 and 7, you will observe the multidimensional role of introspection and self-assessment, played in the field of one's career management and projection of one's destiny with its strong correlation with one's personal attributes of both positive and negative types. Chapters 8 and 9 reveal how introspection enables one to become an awakened and enlightened person and offers scope for becoming a true achiever against heavy odds and adversities.

Finally, as a part of the self-guidance process, I have given in Chapter 4, five directly loaded questions which are addressed to career seeking candidates to answer honestly, sincerely and truthfully. Besides, a format is also enclosed separately as Annexure 2 to Chapter 3 for one to write one's self-assessment and self-appraisal report in precise terms for one's ready reference. It will certainly form a sound base for building your career plan and drive one to endeavour for positively achieving success in one's lifetime objectives.

R.M. Onkar (Lt. Col. Retd)

Introduction

Selection of a proper career is the vital concern of any individual with a strong desire to achieve growth and prosperity which should naturally emerge in future. As such, there is a growing career consciousness and intense desire in students and serving candidates to seek assistance and advice from available outside sources. Parental advice-cum-guidance-cum-pressure plays no doubt a decisive role in influencing their wards to adopt particular careers because they have their own preconceived ideas and expectations about the bright future of their wards. They believe that their wards would be able to achieve growth and prosperity and perhaps meet their unfulfilled desires. Unfortunately, they remain unaware, unmindful and unconcerned about their potential, abilities, aptitude and interest. The need therefore exists in order to address the basic issue of career guidance and selection in order to enable them to make a proper and productive choice which should positively result in success and bring benefits in their life.

It is strongly felt that you have to fully get involved in the process. You have to play a vital role in approaching and frankly expressing about yourself. In other words, you are essentially required to know about your personal qualities or attributes and particularly about the strong and weak or positive and negative or good and bad points, and also likes and dislikes. It simply leads to the theme of Knowing Thyself.

When this theme is examined, it pertains to the important processes of introspection and self-assessment. There is a direct method from many available for practically implementing it. In this method, you are directly involved for carrying out the process. What it basically needs you to have total honesty, sincerity, truthfulness, clarity and frankness while examining and assessing your own attributes of both positive and negative types in order to come to a positive and meaningful conclusion.

It is well known that various careers/courses/services need different personal qualities in different proportions and levels. You should therefore do self-assessment and self-appraisal honestly and dispassionately before making a final choice for a particular career from many available careers and courses. Such an approach of doing proper detailed homework is strongly advocated in order to make the choice of a right career/course so as to avoid putting a square peg in a round hole. In this respect, parents should advise their wards to do such homework and give them freedom for exercising their choice instead of pressurising and persuading them for adopting a particular career/course.

While in service, you are likely to be promoted to different levels of positions and ranks during your service period. It is obviously based on your performance and achievement of objectives for your organisation. It becomes the decisive factor in determining your promotions to higher ranks. Consequently, your Annual Confidential Report (ACR) is written by your superior officers who watch, observe and assess your visible performance. You demonstrate your nature, character, behaviour, abilities, professional skills, talent and a host of other qualities such as loyalty, dedication, diligence, temperament, firmness, vision etc. This is the direct result of your personal attributes of both positive and negative types which affect your demonstrative performance and achievement of the end objectives.

It is pointed out that external factors such as parental care, education, upbringing, environment, relations, yoga/meditation, etc., do play a significant role in causing your effective self-development. You have to be responsive, adaptive and receptive to them for assimilating their positive effects in your nature, character, behaviour and personality. Besides, you should follow a set of steps and measures as given in Chapter 4 as the part of self-development programme. It certainly helps to augment your certain positive attributes and control certain negative attributes. It becomes a right step in the direction of achieving success in your career and lifetime activities.

You have to often face placement agencies for interviews while seeking an employment. It is needless to emphasize that you have got to meticulously prepare and submit your personal resume along with your application. You should know how to comprehensively prepare your resume (C.V.) in which you should skilfully highlight the strong points of your nature and character along with emphasis on your professional skills and talent. You should also know that there are three main traits or aspects of your self such as Personality, Aptitude and Motivation which are carefully observed and examined through a series of questions by the interviewing members. They would also like to know whether you are aware about the needs and expectations of your employer. Their assessment and judgement about your suitability are broadly based on these three main human traits which are believed by the Human Resource Department to be necessary for making a significant positive contribution to the organisation or industry.

The objective of this book is to offer you a direct method for carrying out self-assessment and self-appraisal in order to know your capacity, capability, abilities and their limits so as to enable you to exercise proper care, caution and discretion in making a choice and pursuing of a proper career and subsequently achieving promotions therein. At the same time, the Advisor or Counsellor whom the candidates approach for advice or counseling, needs to know the basis and method for giving proper guidance and should have some ethics to follow. You would like to know the concept of destiny and its correlation to success or failure through your personal attributes of positive and negative types. Parents also need to follow certain guidelines and understand the implications of forcing their choice on their wards.

The process of self-assessment is quantified and presented on the platter for your reference and appropriate action along with a road map of steps for your self-development. It is further extended to conduct self-appraisal in the form of the SWAIT Analysis, like management people do, about your strength, weakness, aptitude, interest and threat areas in the form of opportunities and time. While efforts are made to state various fields and areas of different available careers/courses/services and the technique for ascertaining your interest areas, its scope is restricted to enable you to do positive and constructive homework. Career selection is then left to you as per the need as felt by you from various aspects and angles which are discussed in Chapter 2. It is of course pointed out that you should carry out the process of Introspection, aelf- assessment and self-appraisal honestly, sincerely, truthfully and dispassionately.

As regards your destiny, it is a mystic aspect of your life. Success or failure is in fact found to be linked with your personal attributes which drive and motivate you to act or not to act at opportune times in life, thereby establishing a close correlation between them. While elaborating on the concept of the destiny, it is pointed out that your destiny is decided at the time of your birth as the result of influence from combination of the cosmic/ heavenly and earthly forces as existing at the time of birth and your genetic factor. You may therefore find an indirect answer to success or failure, finally and effectively attributable to your personal attributes which are in fact related to destiny and generally and finally held responsible in the most simplified form.

The entire subject in this book is divided and discussed in nine chapters apart from the Introduction.

There are four Annexures which illustrate various aspects of these chapters in the detailed form. Incidentally, each Annexure is attached to its chapter in order to maintain continuity in reading and understanding.

Since emphasis is given on practicing a direct method for self-assessment, a comprehensive detailed list of positive and negative attributes is given in Annexure 1 to Chapter 2 along with proper operating notes. Technique for writing your Person Performance Report (PPR) is given in the Annexure 4 to the Chapter 6 for carrying out your own honest, sincere and truthful assessment. In fact, it brings out your abilities, talent, potential, capabilities, performance and personal traits. Its unique feature is that it becomes your true projection and reveals such information of your personality that has direct impact on your career, promotions and advancement. It forewarns you about your negative features and need for its timely correction. You are able to write your own Self-Assessment and Self-Appraisal Report for which a format is given in the Annexure 2 to Chapter 3. Finally, a consoling note is prudently enclosed as an Annexure 3 to Chapter 4, advocating introspection to those who especially meet failure at the threshold of their career, like failure in passing higher secondary examination.

It is seen that issues of your personality development and career advancement are placed at the centrestage and the technique of introspection and self-assessment is fully illustrated with its multi-faced applications for improving your service career prospects. It probes into your career-oriented destiny and reveals your key and focal role in the success or failure of achieving your lifetime objectives.

It should be remembered that Introspection and self-assessment play highly important and effective role in enabling you to manage your career and achieve its advancement. It also enables you to project your image and potential for marketing in the competitive employment market. After all, it offers you a professional edge and unlocks the hidden treasure of your remarkable and exceptional qualities that make you an achiever in life against heavy odds and adversities. You have a chance to get awakened from the slumber of ignorance about yourself and gain knowledge and wisdom that lead you to empowerment and enlightenment. Your destiny remains no longer a mystic entity but you try to understand it in a more pragmatic and rational manner.

Thus, it is observed that introspection and self-assessment definitely have multidimensional feature that makes you a highly effective enriched performer. Consequently, you are naturally entitled to promotions. Your knowledge, wisdom and maturity become productive and meaningful.

Finally, it is strongly hoped that this book serves as a practical guide to students in career selection, to the parents for guiding their wards, to the business man for starting his enterprise/ industry, trade or self-employment, to the person who is already in service, to the employers who have to promote employees to higher positions of responsibilities and to the employees who seek higher promotions. Thus, the book will go a long way to offer you effective advice, guidance and counselling in managing and advancing your career and also to those who wish to scale the heights of promotions and reach higher positions of status and authority. So, don't miss it and remain without it, otherwise you will miss a personal, reliable, trustworthy and knowledgeable guide who has a strong potential to take you to a bright future.

Contents

1

Understanding of Introspection and Self-Assessment

SCOPE

1. What is the present level of understanding about introspection?
2. Should you only have blind faith and gut feelings while dealing with your career / business?
3. What is the need for knowing about yourself?
4. What are the present techniques available for knowing about you?
5. What is the mechanism for doing Introspection?
6. What do you mean by Direct Personal Method? How is it convenient for practicing Introspection?
7. What is the role of time factor in the process of Introspection?
8. What is the multi-dimensional role of Introspection in your service career?

Preamble

At the outset, I do not intend to deal with that subject of introspection which has apparently got philosophical and spiritual profile and background. In the spiritual introspection, you are advised to look inwards within yourself and look for your origin, composition, existence and other metaphysical aspects. You should also examine their correlation with outside world where cosmic and earthly forces are active and potent in influencing entire nature and its living creatures. This philosophical and spiritual presentation of an introspective process discourages its acceptance by the youth under the pretext of being a mystic, occult and serious subject. They strongly feel that it is not within their capabilities to understand and practise. Further, they hardly know its utility and application in their present service career. As a result, there is general aversion with a usual remark that it is too early to do introspection and it should better be left to their retirement periods and old-age activities. Hence, my scope of dealing with the subject is limited to its concept, understanding and technique in the context of the youth and their service careers with emphasis on those aspects which normally pertain to their easy comprehension, interest, objectives and applications. In this respect, I have specifically included chapters which highlight the multidimensional role of introspection in different domains of human life. Besides, practical technique is offered for carrying out introspection and self-assessment at any time of your choice and convenience without assistance from any outside agency. So, you find that the subject which basically appears to be mystic is brought to your doorstep in a practical manner with emphasis on its direct application to your service career without having philosophical and spiritual frills and overtones.

Present Scenario

Introspection is today a much-talked single-word subject. Whenever a failure occurs on political front or academic side or anywhere, high profile leaders advocate their parties or students or candidates to do introspection in order to find out the reasons for their failures. Frequent-off the-cuff references are profusely made to this word introspection which receive patient and obedient response from the audience. Naturally, the leaders look for the results of their important advice, so seriously given to their followers. Now, the confusion starts as to what exactly to do and how to execute this valuable advice in practice. They remember that the advice was limited to do introspection but nobody told them how to do it. Nobody has gone deep into its various aspects except making frequent references to this word. Nobody has even bothered to show them a way for actually doing introspection. Thus, the practical aspect is totally ignored and found lacking in such an open advice. As a result, no benefits are actually accrued. On the contrary, a confused state of mind continues without anyone making serious efforts to definitely know about its practical aspects. This is a peculiar and strange situation where a lot of importance is given to introspection but unfortunately, it remains the least understood, practised and followed advice because of ignorance and unawareness about its practical aspects.

It is observed that students and job seeking candidates are blindly going for the careers and jobs that come their way. There is no deliberate thinking and appraisal in order to find out what job or career will suit them best and eventually become productive and prosperous for them in future. In fact, there is no proper mechanism which can be applied for ascertaining the suitability of a particular career. It is also found that the candidates are not aware about specific techniques for carrying out such a study and appraisal by them. Besides, people are not aware about the potential advantages of introspection whenever they carry it out in the self-addressed mode which invokes their total personal involvement in the entire process where they remain at the centre stage as main actors.

Blind Faith and Efforts

There is another aspect of introspection. People generally focus their attention on external factors for achievement of success or occurrence of failure. They believe that external forces and agencies primarily influence the outcome of their mission and career. They have very little to contribute except doing their job and complying with the instructions and orders. Unfortunately, they are not aware that they play a highly effective and focal role in performance of their jobs and careers. As such, they alone consequently become responsible for gaining success or failure in their lifelong events.

Besides, it is observed that certain class of people has misconceptions about their personal confidence and merits. They claim credit for success without trying to understand why it has come to their way. They are also the first persons to lay the blame at the doorsteps of others for their failure or loss by saying that the result was due to the factors beyond their control. They also apportion the blame to their destiny without realising their own faults and mistakes. They firmly and blindly believe that they personally have nothing to contribute towards failure or loss in their mission but they are ever-ready to take credit for any success without realising their actual contribution.

With this type of scenario and treatment being given to introspection by its advocates and advisors, there is an urgent need to seriously take up the subject of introspection and specifically examine it for application to the service and business careers. On deep and deliberate consideration, it is observed that introspection has many multifarious aspects and functional domains which have got important bearing and influence on human life. In fact, its scope is so vast that it is found to practically cover every aspect of your life events and activities. Naturally, **introspection becomes your valuable and highly useful means for steering the progress of your career because it substantially enhances the power and potential of your personality and performance**. In this respect, introspection is found more useful to persons young and middle age for fulfilling future aspirations than to old age persons when there reach the maturity or retirement stage.

Meaning of Introspection

Plainly speaking, it is a self-addressed exercise for carrying out your inner search in order to find out information about your qualities, potential, abilities, nature and character. It is basically a process which enables you to look deep within yourself and deliberate on your personal strengths, weaknesses, talent and aptitude. You also take a look at your body features and health and ascertain your body movements, habits, conduct, look and endurance. You turn your attention to yourself and see its reflection in mirror as your image. It is simply a method in which you seriously and honestly consider about your self and critically examine various aspects of your inner and outer personality. Naturally, it becomes a self-practiced exercise of discovering your potential, power, nature, talent and personality.

MECHANISM

How is it possible?

How are you going to do it? Is it practical? These are the natural questions which are arising in your mind.

In fact, introspection pertains to the basic process of questioning yourself and trying to seek honest and truthful answers. In a way, you pose questions to yourself about your personal qualities of both positive and negative types and find out whether you possess them or not. You may ask certain introspective questions and find out their answers in terms of Yes or No. Thus, you are able to get an idea about your potential and power in the form of these answers which eventually become your manifestation in physical and subjective forms, both representing your outer and inner features. It should be remembered that introspection seeks an interactive dialogue with your Self for revealing true information about your Self. Here, you are communicating with yourself in an interrogative mode. So, you are responsible to your Self. Obviously, your honesty, sincerity and truthfulness to your Self will bring out a very realistic picture about your self. Introspection offers true, correct and pragmatic perspective of your Self. In this process, **you are an actor, performer, thinker and judge.** Thus, introspection has its seed in your Self-oriented efforts and action which are entirely and exclusively directed to your Self for seeking valuable information about you. Introspection is akin to your sincere and honest efforts to fathom and discover valuable treasure of your total personality.

As you get the basic information about possession of your qualities/attributes of both positive and negative types, it demands that you should have enough patience and tolerance to know both sides of positive and negative information and you should remain fair and unbiased especially when you are assessing your negative aspects. Such a self-addressed and self-centric exercise generates feedback information which you can use for correcting the direction of your career's course.

It should be noted that introspection demands your exclusive time which should be devoted from your busy schedule of activities. You should set aside some time for your Self and that is your right to do when you are doing so much in the interest of your career and family members. In fact, it becomes your self duty to patiently and calmly sit down for a few minutes if not an hour for carrying out introspection. During this period, you should exclusively think about yourself by looking deep inside your inner Self. This activity can be carried out along with yoga and meditation which are prominent self-practiced exercises. What is the most important is to turn your attention to yourself and commence questioning in an introspective mode and seek self-specific information which has bearing and influence on your nature, character, talent, personality and performance. In any way, this turns out to be an exercise to "know and underst and thyself" Now, the next question is—**Why should I know about my self?**

NEED FOR UNDERSTANDING YOUR SELF

It is logical and relevant as to why you should know about your Self. What are the benefits which are derived by knowing about your Self ? Does it motivate you to work and perform better ? Will it make a difference to your style of working and performance? Now, it becomes imperative at an early stage of your service career to ask certain pertinent and relevant questions to yourself such as:

a) Who am I ? What is my background? What was the status of my parents and place of birth? What were the environmental conditions existing during my childhood? How could I get my primary and secondary education? How did I get the support for my higher education? What was my academic performance in annual examinations? Incidentally, information which you seek by this way of questioning is required to establish your handicap or opportunity level. If you have to bear a handicap level, it means that you have to initially make additional efforts to come up to the level playing field with others while competing. So, it speaks for your strength, power, potential, talent and perseverance that become the plus factors of your nature and character.

(b) Am I clear about my dream and vision pertaining to a career which I wish to pursue? Does it have any relevance to my aspirations?

(c) Do I bear specific likes and dislikes? What are the sensitive and weak areas of my personality?

(d) Am I greedy, selfish and envious? Am I temperamental or cool headed person? Do I carry a positive mindset?

(e) What are my potential and capabilities for rising in life? How high can I reach? Does it remain an affordable and reachable target for me?

(f) What are the specific and prominent positive and negative aspects of my nature, character and personality? Are they adequate to cause my progressive promotions and career advancement?

(g) What are my limitations that set levels for rise and fall in my service career or business undertakings? In other words, what is my bottom line for commencement and where should I stop in my personal growth and prosperity?

(h) What types of controls, measures and support are possible for me to implement for monitoring and effecting checks on the course of my career growth?

(i) How should I find out the road map for my self-improvement and development?

These are normal and highly relevant questions, arising in your personal life pertaining to your nature, career and its growth. They are immensely important for carrying out self-assessment, appraisal and review especially when periodic failures or losses occur in your life.

Ambition

It is always good to have an ambition and the strong will power, required to achieve it in life by fair and reasonable means. Pursuit of an ambition is considered a noble, dignified and justifiable task. It gets appreciation and support from your relatives, friends and patrons. What it needs is to set limit for lower and upper levels beyond which one should not be over ambitious. In other words, one should know where to stop and not to cross the limit despite favorable or compelling reasons and circumstances. In fact, on achieving the upper limit of your career growth and prosperity, you should better apply breaks to your attitude of temptation and greed. Here, you should become cautious and look for incoming direct or indirect warning signals about forthcoming adverse consequences to occur in many ways at any time. In case, you fail to take its cognisance and still pursue, it is entirely your responsibility for facing the front and bearing its consequences.

Techniques for Introspection

The main purpose of this technique is to find out and reveal information about your self. The quality and accuracy of information depend upon its validity and rationality in light of the assumptions which are normally made for relevance of the results. Various techniques that are available for finding out information about your self are given as under:

a) Chinese Astrology
b) Nine-Star Astrology
c) Four-Pillar Destiny
d) Indian and Western Astrology
e) Palmistry and Face Reading
f) Direct Personal Method

The first three techniques belong to the art of **FENG SHUI** and are mainly based on knowing the energy envelope of an individual from his birth data like year, month, day, and time of birth. During the course of discussion on this subject, it is seen that the heavenly and earthly forces which exist at the time and place of birth play an important role in structuring the nature and character of a human being.

The birth data of persons differ and this difference clarifies the interesting aspect of variation in human nature, character and personality which are widely different and distinctly perceptible. In this context, these techniques reveal information about persons only when asked for and receive information from FENG SHUI experts who refer to various books, charts and Chinese calendar in response to the direct queries. Here, individuals play no role except furnishing their birth data and verifying the result about its validity.

Indian Astrology, Palmistry, Face Reading and Numerology belong to the oriental systems and reveal certain attributes of human nature from horoscope and hand study. Here, you are required to furnish your birth data and refer to an astrologer or palmist for knowing about you. You have no role to play in the process and accept the information without any reservation. You can cross check and verify information from other equally competent and experienced persons.

It is not proposed to discuss these methods which are of indirect nature. You have to approach and request a specialist. He works on your request and after receiving birth data, he submits his assessment and prediction.

Direct Personal Method

It is proposed to discuss only the direct personal method in which an individual has to act and actually participate directly and honestly. It is a self-assessment technique by advocating you to look within your Self and find out your own attributes of both positive and negative types from a comprehensive list of personal attributes which is given in the Annexure 1 to the next chapter. Their relationship with various career aspects is also illustrated. This is an objective and fairly effective method wherein you as an individual are personally involved and do an objective assessment of your self in sincere, honest and truthful manner. You simply ask yourself a question whether you possess a particular attribute or quality after fully understanding its meaning. After giving a serious thought, you may say yes or no. If the answer is yes, then the next question, you ask—How much or what is its level? After the process is over, you tabulate the result with a certain number of yes and no with its quantum level stated against each attribute. It is a simple self-addressed exercise which can be quietly and patiently carried out by you on yourself. In this process, you need to be realistic in assessing yourself and remain unbiased and unprejudiced in order to avoid overestimation and inflation of your positive attributes.

Consequently, the direct method is used for carrying out introspection. You don't need to remember any complex technology except you need to carry a comprehensive list of human attributes / qualities of both positive and negative types.

You have to understand the meaning of each attribute and see if it is applicable to you. In fact, the entire range of attributes is broadly divided in three categories as essential, desirable and optional. At the initial stage, you should worry about the essential attributes. Other types come to play their role when you start getting promotions and reach senior and high level ranks. This aspect is discussed in the next chapter.

TIMING

Introspection should be occasionally carried out as a part of ritual or habit. You should not wait for any special occasion or till it becomes essential and inevitable. When it is developed as a part of your habit, it becomes quite productive and pre-emptive for any adverse situation as you are able to timely apply counter measures and take corrective action before an unforeseen thing occurs. Thus, you remain prepared and consciously aware to face and overcome snags and obstacles whenever they occur in your mission. It eventually leads you to success or at least enables you to minimise the losses on account of failure in your mission.

Another occasion when you should sincerely do introspection is on the occurrence of a failure or loss in the first mission of your career. This could be your failure in the board level examination or interview or enterprise or business or loss of first selection level promotion in service. You should be wise and prudent to find out as to what has gone wrong and where you have committed mistakes or slipped over important parameters and your judgment. You should sincerely and honestly review your performance and identify the slippages and genuine causes. If it reveals commission of your mistakes, you should honestly and frankly admit them. In fact, you can now adopt corrective measures with proper guidance, advice and cautious approach in your second and subsequent attempts. The important point to note here is your willingness, frankness and wisdom to honestly admit your mistakes and errors and avoid tendency to blame the outside agencies and their forces. Introspection whenever undertaken with a positive mindset under these circumstances certainly helps and guides you for gaining success thereafter.

It is also found that certain class of persons keeps trying and pursuing their careers or missions without carrying out any deliberation on causes of their successes or failures. They do not introspect for their continued failures or losses. They keep on committing the same mistakes and wrong deeds without considering any change in their approaches and methods. Besides, they do not show any interest and willingness to consult other competent and experienced persons and timely seek their advice for guidance and proper action. They eventually believe in their bad destiny and attribute failures to existing poor planetary conditions (*Grahdasha*). Such persons totally lay down their hands and finally surrender to circumstances and accept failure as a part of their bad destiny and result of the cursed horoscope.

In this ongoing process and past events, an individual has obviously lost much valuable time of his prime youth till he realises through the medium of horoscope that something is wrong. Here, an individual should pause and deliberate in a rational manner. Introspection offers a powerful and effective means which is strongly advocated in this book as an important self-corrective process for your acts of commissions and omissions in life. There is, of course, need to develop this habit of carrying out introspection so that you can pursue it without any outside impulse and interference. In fact, whenever you meet or perceive a loss or failure in your mission or experience restlessness and instability in your decision, you should realise the urgent need for introspection. The tendency to blame outside forces should be discouraged as a bad habit. **Your fingers should firstly be directed towards yourself.** Your mind should be focused in order to ascertain the causes which may arise from your certain negative qualities and why you failed to realise their impact. Hence, the process of introspection becomes important and critical for self-assessment. It awakens an individual to realise his shortcomings and obviously sets his urge in motion for taking remedial and preventive measures. As a result, he is now prepared to face any adverse situation with courage, strength and boldness. These are important offshoots from the simple act of introspection.

Multi-dimensional Role of Introspection

Introspection is a self-addressed exercise which initiates a process within yourself for discovering yourself in a realistic and positive manner. Human life has several dimensions which cover several life events and activities. They are taking place in a certain deterministic manner. Consequently, you have to function and perform under different conditions. As you know yourself much better and that too realistically, you can take up and manage your service career boldly and confidently. You can now face risks and challenges of your service career with courage, strength and high morale. This basic transformation in your attitude and mindset has wide ramifications in covering various aspects of your life where introspection plays very significant and powerful role in different forms. The multidimensional aspect of introspection may be treated as its functional role in different applications. Let us take a look at those different areas where introspection is found to play an important role for:

a) Guidance in selection of a proper job and career which should match your potential, aptitude and IQ level.

b) Preparing and boldly facing public interviews, group discussions and negotiations.

c) Performance of a job according to the employer's expectations.

d) Effective development of your real positive personality.

e) Effective management of your service career.

f) Self-Awakening and Enlightenment for enriching your career and empowering your life.

g) Revealing your potential, strength and power for successfully marching towards your destiny.

h) Becoming an Achiever against heavy odds and adverse conditions

Incidentally, you will get detailed information about these roles of introspection in Chapters 5 to 9 of this book.

The details of personal attributes and their relationship with various career aspects are illustrated in Chapter 2.

2

Self-Assessment of Your Qualities/Attributes

SCOPE

1. What is the identity of a person?
2. What is the nature and classification of human qualities?
3. What are the different aspects of personal qualities?
4. How are they related to different aspects of human life?
5. What is the comprehensive list of positive and negative qualities and its classification for different functions?
6. How will you prepare your own Personal Attribute Profile?
7. How are your qualities manifested? What is the correlation of your qualities with your mind?
8. What is a mindset? How is it formed?
9. What is your talent? How is it correlated with your personal qualities?
10. What is the synergetic aspect of personal qualities?

Identity of a Person

You know that two persons are not alike. They significantly differ in their body features such as face, nose, eyes, forehead, etc. As such, each person carries his identity by virtue of his physical features which are prominently visible to naked eyes at the first glance. Obviously, these physical features of a person have mainly become a powerful and significant source for establishing his identity for recognition in private as well as public for various applications such as to be a witness, appearing for an interview, etc.

Besides the physical identity, there is another way of establishing the identity of a person. It is called **Qualitative Identity** which is based on the qualities of a person. Of course, it becomes an invisible but adequately perceptible identity which is undoubtedly significant in the sense that no two persons are identical in their personal qualities. As a result, they significantly differ in their nature, character, behaviour, mindset and attitude. They act differently and react differently to external stimuli. This is possible because they possess different qualities of both positive and negative types in varying strengths.

Thus, persons are identified not only by their physical body features but also by their qualities / attributes which are integral part of their inner selves. Eventually, they become responsible for their nature, character, behaviour, relation and performance in a highly perceptible manner. Now, you observe and recognise the nature and character of a person but you hardly see and realise the source which prompt and force a person to act and function in an individualistic manner that eventually becomes his personal identity on a qualitative basis.

The qualities as inherently possessed by persons are very important and effective parameters because they are their prime shakers and movers. Consequently, they make a person active, dynamic or static in his conductive, functional and performing role. Here, the physical body features do not play any role in forming the nature, character and behaviour of a person except that they may become indicative and informative to an expert for assessment and prediction. In fact, they have no direct role in conditioning the nature and character of a person but a few of them indirectly act in consonance with the nature, character and behaviour of a person. This is evident in the form of an individual's habit, mannerism and style while conducting and interacting with others.

Since it is the fact that persons have different nature, character, behaviour, talent and since they are the direct offshoots of their individual qualities, the study of personal qualities and their quantitative assessment becomes a significant exercise for introspection. In fact, introspection enables you to silently and patiently peep deep within yourself and observe, examine and analyse your inherent qualities which you possess since your birth. It becomes a self-addressed exercise of taking a close look at yourself and critically examining the unseen valuable treasure of your qualities which effectively govern you and steer your career course in a specific direction.

Nature and Classification of Qualities

Human qualities are mainly divided in two parts, one of positive type and another of negative type. Qualities of positive type improve, support and enhance any process of life while negative types obstruct, inhibit and retard the process and its progress. Consequently, positive qualities help a person to move forward and achieve success while negative qualities retard the progress and push a person backward, thereby causing failure or loss in his mission.

There are innumerable qualitative features which are significantly identified in both positive and negative qualities. They pertain to different aspects of mankind and have different functional domains in human life. As such, they are classified under the following heads:

a) Nature and character.
b) Relations, behaviour and conduct.
c) Education and upbringing.
d) Performance and activities.
e) Business and self-employment.
f) Leadership.

All the qualities of a person are broadly placed in the above categories of functional domains. Each domain has different aspects and causes different effects on human life. There is always overlapping of certain qualities over certain functional domains. As such, there is no strict compartment-wise division in their requirements over different contact centres of human life. Of course, there are certain essential qualities which are basically required for undertaking any career / service. The remaining qualities become desirable and optional and their requirement is only felt whenever you want to pursue a special service or a career on the growth ladder with promotional prospects to senior and higher appointments and posts with rank and status. Let us now take a close look at various qualities / attributes as required for different domains of human life.

Personal Qualities / Attributes

Personal qualities demonstrate the basic nature and character of a person. They are an inherent part of the human beings and endowed to them at the time of their birth which includes the data of year, month, date and time of the birth. Most of them are gifted to them from the heavenly and earthly energy sources arising from positions of the heavenly bodies such as planets, sun, which are moving in their respective orbits in the Zodiac. Others are passed on to them genetically from their parents. The origin of the personal attributes is very important as it determines the destiny of a person in his lifetime. In fact, a person carries these personal attributes as an imprint of his identity right from the day of his birth and it is possible to read them from his birth data such as year, month, day and time of birth, and also from his body features such as hand and face. These personal attributes are classified under five heads as under:

a) **Mental—Related to Mind**: such as Ambition, Will power, Tenacity, Firmness, Intuition, Determination, Integrity, Responsiveness. Awareness.

b) **Emotional—Related to Emotions and Feelings**: such as Sensitivity, Sincerity, Anger, Daring, Consciousness, Temperament, Morality, Politeness, Assertiveness, Keenness, Tolerance.

c) **Psychic—Related to Psychology**: such as Maturity, Stability, Outlook, Initiative, Consistency, Passiveness, Extrovert / Introvert, Sulkiness, Mindset, Critical, Adamancy, Stubborness.

d) **Intellectual—Related to Thinking Power of Mind**: such as Intellect, Logic, Expression, Creativity, Memory, Reasoning, Ingenuity.

e) **Physical—Related to Body and its Structure**: such as Personality, Stamina, Capacity, Tenderness, Appearance, Bearing, Endurance, Health.

Although mental, emotional and psychic qualities may be broadly classified under one head, they are listed here separately to differentiate the granulites in their features and levels.

It is believed that first three types of the above stated personal qualities are inborn and endowed to us at the time of birth like software in the computer. The last two types are passed on to us genetically through the hereditary channels attributed to the mother or father or both and sometimes extended to grand-parents. These personal attributes serve as the base and are essentially dominating our career / service.

Qualities for Relation and Behaviour

The attributes related to this aspect are behavioural and interactive in nature. They are demonstrated while dealing and working with different types of people in service period and thereafter. These outside people may belong to your home as spouse, parents, brothers and sisters or society as friends, neighbours or workplace as subordinates, seniors and colleagues. While dealing with such a broad spectrum of the people belonging to different strata of the society and work culture, it is important to see how you behave and interact with them. Ultimately, it affects your relationship in the form of friendship, attachment, comradeship, dependability and team spirit which are important factors for forming bonds and a close-knit family and organisational structure. It matters a lot for removing stress and strain of your high responsibilities and bringing to you peace, happiness and contentment which consequently boost your energy and morale for working more effectively and efficiently. Here lies the key for achievement of your life mission as well as that of the organisation to which you belong. These attributes are categorised as under:

a) Family type—Leading to behaviour at home.
b) Society type—Leading to behaviour with friends, neighbours.
c) Office type—Leading to behaviour and working with subordinates, colleagues and seniors.
d) Community type—Involving religion, politics, educational institutions, business/work places.

These relationship oriented qualities which have important bearing on human relationship are highlighted as under:

— Sensitivity, Cooperation, Honesty, Credibility, Expression, Listening, Gentleness, Politeness, Tactfulness, Responsibility, Support, Willingness, Communication, Softness, Patience, Responsiveness, Dependability, Loyalty.

The above list of qualities is indicative of various factors and facets of human nature involved in dealing with people of different categories. The outcome of your behaviour will depend upon the response of the other party and situation, you are facing at a particular time and place.

Attributes for Education and Upbringing

During your early stage of growth, you go to school and colleges and acquire basic and high level education. Here, you pass different levels of academics and demonstrate your performance in the form of different grades achieved in final annual examinations. You attend different professional job oriented courses and achieve skills for performance in different trades. Now, the proficiency and grade you achieve in the education and professional training depends upon your interest, hard work and talent and how you response in a positive or negative manner. At the same time, you have to face different types of working conditions and environments which may be conducive, favourable and opportunistic to you or they may be adverse, unfavourable and unhealthy for your real upbringing and studies. Now, it depends upon you how you respond to these outside conditions and still achieve your proper education and professional skills with proper exposure to the ethics and culture while growing up. For this purpose, you need to possess certain qualities which should enable you to achieve proper education and upbringing. They are stated as under:

— Responsiveness, Comprehension, Tenacity, Determination, Firmness, Initiative, Confidence, Vision, Ambition, Hard work, Diligence, Tolerance, keenness, Obedience, Politeness, Humility, Openness, Dedication, Perseverance, Inquisitiveness, Concentration, Devotion, Respectfulness.

The attributes related to this aspect successfully motivate and drive you towards your objective and ambition which can only be achieved by acquiring proper education and professional skills.

As they pertain to you, they form part of your personal qualities. Some of them may be developed under advice and guidance from parents, teachers and counsellors. However, it needs your intrinsic response, clear vision, intense ambition and firm determination for adoption to educational domain.

Performance-Oriented Attributes

These qualities are responsible for performance of an individual and achievement of success in life. They are also responsible for growth of career and business. This performance could be seen in various fields such as academics, business, service, office, home where what matters is the end result and that is success of the mission. Emphasis is always on achieving long term gains although short term gain also matters under certain circumstances for maintaining the momentum and progress in performance.

Performance is basically a demonstrative and result oriented phenomenon where success can be assessed quantitatively and qualitatively. It is continuously observed by your superiors and watched intently and minutely by your subordinates, juniors and colleagues. In this respect, apart from success of an individual, what matters finally is the success of an organisation or family as a whole to which you belong.

Hence, attributes which are responsible for giving effective, efficient and visible performance of a person in any service are indicated as under:

- Professional knowledge, Responsiveness in Training, Motivation, Managing & Organising Skills, Foresight, Awareness, Team spirit, Communication skills, Adaptability, Dependability, Tactfulness, Flexibility, Sense of Time, Resourcefulness, Initiative, Commitment, Creativity, Responsibility, Loyalty and Integrity.

These performance-oriented qualities are important and seen in your day-to-day activities. Effective and efficient performance of a person is quite considerably influenced by these qualities. In fact, these performance-oriented parameters are assessed and judged by your superior officers for your capabilities and potentialities in delivering good results in service organisation and project work. The relative weightage is given to different parameters in the form of marks by your superiors while writing your Annual Performance Report. These performance oriented qualities are mainly responsible for taking a person up or down the ladder of the career growth where promotions in various ranks are involved during different stages of service periods.

Attributes for Business and Self-employment Services

For effective and successful performance in any business small or large, there is a need for special qualities in a person besides having most of those qualities as stated above. Before doing a business, it is essential that a person should have prior knowledge, exposure and some experience of that business. Besides, a person must have the aptitude for doing a business. There are many complex aspects of a business which mainly include enterprising spirit and drive. These aspects are stated under different heads as under:

a) Professional knowledge about business product, process and market for sale of products and services.

b) Skill and expertise to run and manage a business by an individual or a group of persons.

c) Interaction with workforce and dealing with people of different types such as buyers, sellers, dealers, servicemen and promoters.

d) Awareness about many aspects such as techno-commercial, financial, accounting, competitive, legal, public utility and government tax liabilities.

Since the scope of any business or enterprise includes many activities which cover selling, negotiation, establishing a workplace and running a business, managing people and personalities, getting things done and going ahead, it demands special qualities in a person who proposes to start a business. In fact, it is a separate subject of business management which is covered under an extensive management training course, It is not proposed to dwell into it but mention here those special qualities which have important bearing on success of any business which may be small or large and of any type and at any place. These qualities as stated above cover mainly three aspects of any business and are further amplified with relation to the following:

a) **Reading People**

— Listen and observe patiently, quietly and attentively.

— Talk less, be discreet and stick to the point of your client interest.

- Be patient, calm, composed, frank, truthful, committed and tactful.

b) **Business Operation-oriented**

- Knowledge of business, rules and regulations, product quality and standards.
- Logistics, production skill, financial matters, time schedule compliance.
- Training for operating skill, aptitude and upgrading of workforce.
- Labour and factory laws, sale tax, income tax, local tax and excise rules.

c) **Sale and Market-oriented**

- Persistence and persuasiveness, Sense for timing of market demand, supply and your competitor's activities, awareness about needs, budget, resources and operating environment of the customers and their hierarchical structure for decision making, preparation of tender and contract documents with clarity on payment terms, price, delivery schedule and legal commitments.

Thus, a person, having above qualities which effectively enable him to run a small or large business and also having wide outlook and quick response should undertake a business career. A person who does not possess fully or partially above qualities should never be asked or forced to undertake or switch over to business career as he will be found a misfit and consequently is bound to fail or loose thereby causing economic disaster and loss of money and morale. You may call such failure to have caused or occurred on account of your bad destiny as is commonly and easily understood. The fact however remains in no uncertain terms that failure has taken place because of the paucity of the above- mentioned business-related and oriented qualities in a person who launched business career without doing any introspection and self-assessment for ascertaining his fitness and suitability for that particular business.

Qualities for Leadership

You are required to act as a leader at different levels and lead a group of persons or a team to perform a mission and achieve its success. No organisation can exist without a leader at the top and small functional levels such as divisions and sections. Executives are appointed to function as their heads and are given total responsibility for operations and finally giving specific results. You as a head have to operate and deal with the staff of a small or large numbers having different assignments and responsibilities. It is your exclusive responsibility as a head to get work out of them and achieve the assigned targets. You are also responsible for their training and keeping them updated in professional and management skills. As a result, you as the head lead them to achieve your mission and target. So, you are required to possess leadership qualities as under:

a) Honesty, professional knowledge, initiative and awareness.
b) Sense of duty, time, responsibility and obligation.
c) Respectfulness, selflessness, supportiveness, cooperation.
d) Commitment, dedication and involvement.
e) Will power, firmness, vision, drive and determination.
f) Loyalty, integrity, enterprising spirit and decisiveness.
g) Communication skill, flexibility and adaptability.
h) Motivation and morale-raising skill.
i) Caring and benevolent.

Besides having above leadership oriented attributes, you should play an active role in the following fields of operations.

a) Planning and organising a task.
b) Delegate responsibilities to the staff members and monitor.
c) Control and supervise the work.
d) Support by encouraging, motivating and giving proper training.
e) Evaluate the performance of staff members with proper cost-benefit approach.

Comprehensive List of Attributes for Self-Assessment

To summarise and recapitulate and at the same time to facilitate the process of introspection and self-assessment which needs to be carried out honestly, sincerely, truthfully and conscientiously, a comprehensive checklist of various attributes of both positive and negative types is given in the Annexure 1 to this chapter at the end of the book. Explanation is given in bracket for stating deeper meaning of each attribute where ever possible.

The scope of these attributes covers broadly two categories of persons as under:

a) Career guidance, selection and counselling for those who intend to launch their career or make its beginning after higher secondary or graduate level examinations.

b) Career promotion and advancement for those who are already in service in Government/semi government/ industry and other organisations.

Hence, the following short forms are used in this Annexure against each attribute at the end of the bracket containing its meaning in order to identify their applicability for the type of areas as stated above

a) For Career Guidance and Selection———— CGS

b) For Career Promotion and Advancement————CPA

[Attributes referred to areas under (a) are marked as CGS. Others which are not marked as such are presumed to refer to areas under (b).]

Before you start the exercise of your assessment, you are advised to scan the entire list of attributes as given in Annexure 1 thoroughly and thoughtfully for your specific application and then tick those attributes which you possess and mark ' X ' those attributes which you do not possess. It is not necessary that you try to cover entire attributes for both types of applications at this stage but you may examine the entire list in order to understand and assess your capacity and potential for rise and achievement of your life objectives in future.

Quantitative Assessment

The next step for you is to ask a simple question to yourself: **How much do I possess this quality**? Thus, you would like to carry out quantitative assessment in which the unit of 10 is used as full marks for allotment to each attribute in case you fully possess a particular positive or negative attribute. This is treated as the maximum proportion or the highest level. In case you possess these attributes in different grades or at different proportions or levels, you can use the following differential quantitative scale of marking:

For positive type

— Excellent: +9 Very good: + 7
Good or Moderate or Average: + 5
Weak or Low: + 3,
Nil or None: 0.

For negative type

— Excessive: -9
Very often or Frequent: - 7
Moderate or often or Average: - 5
Low or seldom or sometimes: - 3
Nil or Not at all: 0.

It should be noted that plus marking is used for possessing positive attributes and minus for negative attributes. Besides giving picture of your individual qualities and their corresponding need for various careers, summation of marking on both sides will indicate the overall profile of yourself and your personality. It should however be noted that various careers and courses need different attributes with different levels of marking such as defence services, needing attributes like leadership, loyalty, integrity, dedication, tenacity, besides physical fitness more than other qualities. Please note that high values of negative qualities which are associated with negative signs indicate dominance of negative qualities.

Process

It is thus pertinent to note that the selection and pursuit of personal career is a thoughtful and judicious process and intimately related to possession of qualities as listed and defined above. It is the responsibility of an individual to address issue of career to him and assess his positive and negative or strong and weak points of his nature and personality. A person must go through this introspection process so as to know his capacity and suitability for selecting and adopting a particular career / course in which he should succeed and bring peace and happiness in his later life.

It is pointed out that the personal qualities and their derivatives as additional qualities and stated above are mostly universal in nature. They are therefore found effective while dealing with different situations and operating under different environments. Their scope and applicability are sometimes overlapping and perhaps repetitive. Efforts are however made to identify them as per the need and application and segregated for quick and easy understanding as much as possible.

Observation

As you walk on the way, you see a few stones lying on the ground midway. In case, you stop and intently observe, you take some time before you decide to either throw away the stones or skip over and walk away. Similarly, when you see someone lying on the ground in an injured state, if you stop, you take some time before you decide to either help him or skip away. You daily come across a number of such events. You don't take an instant decision to act but pause a little, think a bit and then decide to take a particular course of action. You go into action mode only after thinking for a moment.

Inference

What does it mean? How does it happen for you to act? It is commonly understood that after receiving a signal from your sensory organ, your brain passes it to your mind and asks which way to act. Now, your mind goes in thinking mode and instructs the brain for specific action after quickly processing which involves instant analysis of the present situation and comparison with the concerned previously stored data in its memory banks. **What does this ongoing inside background process reveal?** Your brain does not take the decision but looks to your mind to decide. Your mind deliberates by thinking and addressing the issue to your Self which is called your Sub-Conscious Mind. Obviously, your inborn qualities and the way they have become part of your subconscious mind decide the structure of your mindset, its thought process and adoption to various background incidents, events and environment while you are perceiving and experiencing them. So, let us discuss the correlation of your mind with your personal attributes for determining how you respond, act and react to outside signals, stimuli and events.

Correlation of Human Mind with Your Attributes

In normal parlance, the human mind is the most active, dynamic and fast working faculty which is capable of thinking, acting and reacting consciously and subconsciously. It is a free, fluid, and flying entity which pervades and rules over all aspects of your life. It is restless and cannot stay on one object. Since it controls your thinking and visualising process, it generates good or bad thoughts and language and drifts you away from your objective. It functions of its own and receives the inputs from the brain and its memory databank. These inputs may assist the mind in analysing its own data received from its own sensing organs. Inputs received from the brain are not always regulatory in nature but advisory and help the mind to take its own decision and transmit its decision signal to the brain for action.

The emotions, feelings and thoughts are integral part of the mind. It is a free lancer. It moves its thoughts and feelings and brings any phenomenon or view on its mental canvas at the lightening speed. At the same time, it swiftly transfers scenes and views from its mental screen. It carries out dreaming consciously or subconsciously.

You come across several career related books. They contain advice and guidance which are exclusively addressed to your mind, asking it to do and act this way and that way and focus for achieving success in your life. Hence, your mind becomes ultimate destination to receive and store such information and act accordingly.

Now, the question is to see how your mind is related to your attributes. Is the mind the sole depository of your entire attributes? or does it represent a whole lot of your attributes of both positive and negative types as possessed by you? These are pertinent questions which need to be deeply and seriously considered.

As you deeply think and analyse this issue, you come to the conclusion that your mind ultimately becomes the single representative of your attributes. In fact, it becomes quite evident that your mind has conceptual presence in your perceptible personal attributes. Your mind is found to work and direct the brain in accordance with the feedback, given by various attributes of both types as possessed by you and the manner in which they are present. Incidentally, the mind does not have any specific physical presence inside your body nor you can physically locate its specific position. Obviously, only way to perceive the presence of your mind is in the form of the treasure of your personal attributes. However the fact is that your attributes cause your mind to think and act in a particular way so that some of them limit its free-flying zone and regulate its functioning in the desired, purposeful and productive direction. They stop your mind going astray. Hence, the role of some of the attributes while influencing the mind is proactive, constructive and controlling in nature.

As personal attributes are endowed to a child at the time of birth, its mind is influenced and starts taking shape through an internal process of interactive nature. As a child grows, its mind also grows and progressively gets influenced by the external factors, events and their forces. The effects so caused on the child's mind remain hidden in stored form and act as its data bank for reference in future. They regulate and cause qualitative changes in the thought process which eventually depends upon the nature of these forces and their timings. Here, the time for acting of the external forces becomes quite important and critical because you as a human being are naturally placed and allowed to grow between the heaven and earth and their powerful cosmic forces act on you forever. It is a matter of separate study. As far as you are concerned, you perceive the intimate and inseparable relationship between your mind and your personal attributes.

Hence, it becomes pertinent and essential that whenever you look around for advice in order to improve and develop yourself, you have to basically address this issue to your attributes meaning thereby to your mind and its working mode. As a result, you come to know your attributes albeit mind only through the process of introspection and self-assessment. Yoga/meditation is one way of many other efforts to realise your positive attributes which enable your mind to concentrate on specific issues and missions.

MINDSET

Before concluding the subject, a few words are added about a person's mindset which is a complex factor of human nature, mainly pertaining to its psychic aspects. It is reflected in peculiar, strange and uncommon behaviour of a person at certain times with slight provocation and sometimes without it too. Since it deals with the mind of a person, it involves his certain mental faculties which cause the person to think, behave and act in that way. It is associated with the thinking of a person which could be positive or negative / right or wrong / optimistic or pessimistic. As a result, this factor assumes importance for consideration of the human nature and behaviour.

It appears that a person derives his mindset right from the day of birth. It becomes evident in behaviour during childhood, young age and after marriage. Such a person receives proper upbringing, education and all types of facilities for proper growth. Despite this, some persons show a negative mindset and behave strangely, especially during their married period. Their outlooks are found negative and obstructive at domestic, family and social events. They react in a strange and unpredictable manner which is quite irritating and causing nuisance and unpleasantness in their personal as well as public life.

It is said that the mindset is genetically inherited by a child at the time of its birth. It is not the father but mother who is said to play an important role in passing mindset to a child. It is also partly believed to be the influence on a child at the time of its birth, coming from combination of the heavenly and earthly cosmic forces, as it would have existed at that time and resulted in causing positive or negative influence on the brain of a child in varying proportion and intensity.

Thus, a person with a positive mindset has always positive approach and attitude. He is optimistic in outlook and reveals a face free from stress, tension and unnecessary worries. Behaviour and thinking of such a person is rational, logical, pleasant and conducive to friendship and comradeship with a strong team spirit for achieving a collective objective.

To amplify the point and further explain its complexities, mindset is also associated with human attitude which also reflects on the function of human mind. It reveals an immediate reaction to an external event irrespective of its nature and magnitude. It is apparent that your mind when it has dominant presence of certain negative attributes will certainly get activated to think and behave in an abnormal and irrational manner without bothering about its consequences. How much family or personal or social life gets adversely disturbed is no consideration to such a person having negative mindset.

Thus, it is pointed out that negative mindset and dominant presence of negative attributes are intimately correlated in behavioural manner. Negative attributes such as being highly adamant, emotional, suspicious, impulsive, introvert, nervous, self-centered and temperamental are responsible to cause such a mindset in a human being whenever level of their presence exceeds a certain limit.

It is already stated that female parent is partly found responsible to pass this factor genetically to a child in the hereditary chain. It is also found that such person receives no doubt good education and high academic qualifications. They read literature and religious books and move around in pious, docile, gentle and cultured society. They find their life partner equally gentle, loving, rational and docile. Notwithstanding, their mental approach remains negative and irrational on occurrence of minor events of their dislike.

What is a way out? It is necessary that such persons are made to realise and feel the need for Introspection in order to find out their drawbacks and weak points that are causing them to behave irrationally and damage their image and reputation. Once this person gets into the introspective mood and starts realising and worrying about his image, he will positively be ready to adopt remedial measures. As a result, he may create a balance of both types of attributes at least if not dominance of positive attributes and experience relief from his negative mindset.

It is very important to initiate the process of introspection in persons having negative mindsets. An atmosphere of extreme confidence, mutual trust and cordiality with a touch of affection and care has to be created. You should never be openly critical about the mindset of such persons. The process would be slow but smooth and aim at building the bridge of confidence, mutual trust and respect.

The correlation of mind with human attributes is depicted in a typical flowchart as given below:

Correlation Scenario of Human Mind with Personal Attributes

Your mind

↓

And

↓

Mindset represented by your subconscious mind

↓

Forms

↓

Habits, thoughts and visulisation process

↓

Leads to formation of your

↓

Personal attributes of both positive and negative types

↓

Reflected into your

↓

Nature, character, relations, conduct, behaviour

↓

Affect your

↓

Personality and performance

↓

Manifested through

↓

Action of your brain

↓

By giving operational signals

↓

To your action organs

↓

And

↓

Makes a person active and dynamic

Finally, remember the truth and crux that :

- **Your Real Identity is given out by your Mind.**
- **Your Mind's Identity is indicated by the Personal Qualities you Possess.**
- **Your Personal Qualities consequently determine Your Nature, Character, Relations, Conduct, Behaviour and Performance.**
- **You form Your Habits, Working Style and thinking process according to your Personal Qualities**
- **So, Control your Personal Qualities. In turn, You control your Mind and consequently your Destiny.**

Manifestation of Attributes

Various attributes of both positive and negative types are described and listed in the Annexure 1 to this chapter. Their requirements for various human aspects are also stated for different facets of human life. These attributes are not physical entities. They are not physically observable or visible. Due to absence of the physical touch, how to visualise and perceive these attributes is the real question. Since they relate to human nature, character, behaviour and personality, they may be referred to as functional subjective characteristics whose impact and influence are felt on every human activity whether at home, office or work place. Consequently, its outcome may finally be seen in the form of success or failure. In fact, human nature, character, behaviour and personality are strongly dependant on attributes which may be seen as their mirror projection, having important bearing and influence on human performance and activities.

Human attributes are not visible but strongly perceptible. Although they are integral part of human body, they remain unseen. But, they are basically responsible to enable you to lead your life in a particular way. Many of them play very important role in determining the scope and extent of your nature, character, behaviour and personality. The influence is variant, vibrant and dynamic and generates a lot of derivatives whose need is not ordinarily felt at career selection or initial placement in service but later so as you progress towards your career objectives like promotions and advancement.

Attributes can not be separated from your habits and body movements. They play significant role in conditioning your habits. Similarly, attributes are responsible for building constitution of your mental state and direct your mind to think and act in a particular way. Hence, personal attributes and thinking system and its power can not be separated but operate in a closely correlated and coordinated manner. The study of rules and mechanics of operating system of the human mind is a separate subject with vast scope for discussion..

Another important aspect of your personal attributes is highlighted for having their relationship with emotions, feelings and sentiments which are generally associated with the weaker aspects of human nature. Persons who are emotional, sentimental, sympathetic and sensitive have weak nature, character and personality. Consequently, they slow down the momentum of their activities and struggle. Their spirit and morale become weak for achieving their objectives. As such, they are treated as negative attributes whenever their influence is found to exceed a certain threshold level. In fact, it is desirable to have these attributes within the threshold level as they do play positive, productive and constructive role because of their intimate relationship and association with attributes such as maturity, stability, consistency and restraint.

It is thus seen that our mind, mental state, emotions and feelings are manifested in the form of many personal attributes thereby establishing a close correlation for their visual effects and influence on your life events and their outcome.

Another aspect of attributes is presented here where they are found to release the energy to your sense mechanism and centers of action. Physical activity takes place only after receiving sufficient energy to act. In fact, it is the quantum of energy and timing sequence for its release that determine initiation of your activity and its subsequent sustained level for maintaining and finally achieving progress and completion. For example, attributes like awareness, initiative, ambition, will power, vision when present in an individual are indicators of driving and motivating forces for automatic release of such energies and pushing an individual to act and act spontaneously and responsively. Thus, when people use words in their statements like can, may, if, prefer, they are indicators of slow passage of energy from their attributes. On the other hand, whenever fast or immediate action or direct unambiguous approach or expression takes place, it is an indication of release of high level of proactive energy from your positive attributes for action.

Similar is the case with negative attributes which release negative energy and its level determines ill and adverse effects. Moderate release from such attributes will indicate their sober effect but high release of energy and that too from certain negative attributes like anger, envy will result in causing a damaging effect.

Hence, this close relationship between attributes and action oriented release of energy to your centers of action is another dimension of human nature which should be understood and noted for planning and taking an appropriate action at opportune times.

It is further pointed out that some of the attributes which are entirely and strictly personal are innate and remain uncontaminated by the external sources such as upbringing, education and training. They belong to mental faculties. As such, their response to uptake and assimilate is genuine, natural and spontaneous.

Talent as a Manifestation of Attributes

Abilities for doing particular things are associated with possession of certain attributes which enable and influence you to do that job or career. It is sometimes referred to as talent which indicates the natural skill and aptitude given to you from endowment of positive attributes. Thus, talent becomes another form of providing an open window for looking into human life and discovering natural skill, amounting to attributes endowed to us at the time the birth and developed later by external forces.

Talent is unique to you in the form having plenty of positive attributes which impart you skill and abilities to do and practise various activities. It is expressed in various forms like passing examinations with distinction, performing jobs meticulously and earning promotions and so on.

It is generally observed that some candidates squander their talents by having low ambitions and life expectations and do not bother to have vision and purpose for their life. They are not aware about their talents and high potential, endowed to them from their certain strong positive attributes. When you have purpose, vision and high ambition, your talent is marshalled automatically into action to commence fruitful activities. When you are dedicated to your objectives and aspirations, you will find a way to express your talent through it.

Talent is a latent ability, derived from your positive attributes. So, it is said to be raw and incomplete when it is not aligned with your vision, values and life aspirations. When it is aligned, it can go far off. Certain positive attributes are represented selectively in talents in an integrated form and become possession of individuals. Eventually, it becomes tool for personal gratification. So, talent becomes a natural gift.

Now, talent can not be discovered while working or acting defensively and safely. You have to take risks and chances and fully invest yourself in order to achieve positive results. There are certain indicators for you to practice and look for your talent as under:

a) What you enjoy doing?
b) What you enjoy thinking about?
c) What you enjoy learning about?
d) What you enjoy practicing?

Realisation of your talent is revealed from the quote of few lines by Emily Dickinson:

We never know how high we are
Till we are called to rise
And when, if we are true to our plan
Our statures touch the skies

It is now proposed to express talent as your abilities to perform various purposeful activities of importance, covering organisation, management, learning and academics, earning, and relationship. These are given as the part of the Annexure 1 to this chapter and projected as supplement in order to give further assistance for identifying your attributes of both positive and negative types.

Synergy among Attributes

Various types of both positive and negative attributes are described in the Annexure 1 to this chapter. Each attribute is distinct in nature and function. When you consider human attributes and their functional aspects as a whole, they are not found independent but function according to mutually creative cooperation and support each other for producing tangible results. For example, you are a hard working man. Now, if you have attributes like honesty, sincerity, perseverance in addition to hard work, it gets strength, effectiveness and strong support because of release of additional energies from them to the main attribute which is hard work in this example. Similar is the case with other attributes like confidence and ambition to which we add the effects of attributes such as will power, vision. It is thus seen that there is a close inter-relationship among certain attributes to support and strengthen their main functional roles.. This is called synergy among them which unleashes mutually supportive power in order to enhance and materialise the end results. Positive synergy helps to raise and push forward while negative synergy pulls down in opposite direction thereby causing harm to the progress and development in the mission path. Thus, synergetic influence of certain positive and negative attributes must be taken into account while planning and executing the tasks and finally while analysing and evaluating causes especially of failure or loss in life.

Preparing Attributes' Profile

It is now proposed to guide you to prepare your own attribute profile, consisting of both positive and negative types so that you come to know about yourself in a specific way as well as know the strong and weak points of your nature and character. What is therefore required for you to do is to identify various attributes of both types as applicable to you from the Comprehensive List attached as the Annexure 1 and then place them with their subjective gradations under the above heads with an objective to write your own resume or attributes profile which constitutes your Confidential Personal Report as written by you about yourself. Such a Personal Report, if written honestly, sincerely and truthfully becomes your powerful self-assessment tool to guide and direct you ever for your career selection and development besides enabling you to adopt and apply counter remedial measures for self-improvement. The technique as to how to write your own Confidential Personal Report (C P R) which is normally written annually by your superior officers on your overall performance while in service is described in the Annexure 3 attached to Chapter 6. Here, you come across a classic example of writing your own Confidential Report.

Let us now discuss the impact of these personal qualities on self-appraisal for career selection in the next chapter.

3

Self-Appraisal for Career Selection

SCOPE

1. What types of aspirations do you have from your service career?
2. How do you generalise the entire range of attributes of both positive and negative types for different career prospects?
3 What do you mean by SWAIT Analysis?
4. What are the different types of careers and courses?
5. How do you select a particular career? What are the selection criteria which are adopted in a Selection Mode?
6. How will you prepare your Self-Appraisal Report? What is the advantage of such a report while seeking guidance and counselling?
7. What are the guidelines for seeking proper career advice?
8. What is the decision making process in selection of a career?
9. Are you aware that a career is a game and do you know how to play it?

Human Aspirations and Career

The most important phase of your life occurs when you have to work and pursue a profession which enables you to adequately earn for your survival and decent living. Obviously, you have to become competent to adopt a particular profession which should adequately offer financial support and mentally satisfy you for doing things of your liking and that too with your utmost possible capabilities and resources. For this purpose, you have to acquire basic qualifications and gain some professional training so that you become eligible and competent for proficiently doing a particular job. In fact, this is the elementary and essential step in the direction in which you propose to select and launch your career. It enables you to gain adequate firm base in order to first get an employment in any organisation or industry and then prepare you to perform as per the expectations of your employer. This is the beginning of your career and it entirely remains in your hand to steer it in any direction of your liking and choice. So, it is a significant phase of your career where you have to struggle for making yourself educationally and professionally competent for a particular job and then learn how to properly perform it.

Here, the most important issue is the identification of a career and its relationship with your liking and aspirations which you consciously or subconsciously do feel in your mind while observing different classes, grades and ranks of people in different professions and services. It is also relevant to ascertain whether your career has any direct or indirect connection with your innate aspirations where your aptitude lies in the hidden form. So, this issue of human aspirations should be examined before you look for career guidance and selection.

Human Aspirations/Expectations

As a child, you do not understand much of the life and its objectivity except that you are, at that time, aware of your immediate needs for food, shelter, affection, care and education. As a child grows and sees life and environment around, it starts subjectively perceiving wide range of dimensions of life and proportionately growing needs and getting their feel for existence and survival. In a way, it starts gradually opening the canvas of actual life and its varied aspects before him.

As the process of developing interest centers moves around, you become crazy and crave to realise them in life. These interest centers move around the following objectives:-

a) **Family obligations**
b) **Money, wealth and property**
c) **Religion and social services like non-government organisations**
d) **Relation with family members, friends, colleagues and relatives**
e) **Fame, reputation, recognition and awards**
f) **Work / service / business / production / sales**
g) **Academics / scholar / knowledge / research / teaching**
h) **Power, authority, ruling, control, dominance**
i) **Self-addressed upliftment and spiritual pursuit**
j) **Defence and national services**

These are called human aspirations or life expectations and a human being tries to desire for achieving one or two of them. The above types of interest centres give a wide range of tangible human expectations which an individual tries to accomplish with his attributes. It is you who should keep before yourself any of these objectives before you proceed to select a career / course / service so that the career so selected must have the potential and intrinsic value to offer prospects and realise your aspirations.

Your success or failure in life is assessed on the basis of achievement or non-achievement of any of the above life expectations. All your efforts and pursuit are ultimately directed towards this purpose. It is strange though interesting to observe that you attribute the achievement of your aspiration to your Destiny especially when it is actually related to your abilities and potentialities which enable you to achieve it in your lifetime. In fact, most of you inquisitively refer to astrological predictions, published periodically without making any tangible efforts to look into yourself and do some introspection in order to ascertain whether you do have adequate abilities and potential to achieve them through your nature, behaviour and performance.

Hence, there exists a close relationship among these factors such as attributes, career and life expectations. It is advisable to consider them as a whole package so as to consider their long-term repercussions on life events and finally their success or failure towards the end result.

ATTRIBUTES FOR CAREER PROSPECTS

Before you commence to examine and discuss the impact of human attributes on career and there influence on your destiny, it is proposed to classify them in order to assess their influence and importance on any career and service.

Firstly, you know that there are certain positive attributes which are definitely and essentially required for undertaking any career and service irrespective of its scope, nature and prospects. These are called STAR qualities. They are of general nature but essentially required to be present in a person who tries to seek any career or service. Under this category, they are classified as Essential Attributes such as honesty, sincerity, hard-working, loyalty, dedication awareness, endurance, responsibility, drive and will power.

Besides, there are certain additional qualities, required for specific services such as defence in which additional qualities such as leadership, devotion, integrity, initiative, tenacity, team spirit, ambition and dependability are required. These additional qualities are referred to as the STAR PLUS attributes. According to a need based profile of the attributes as felt actually in practice, the entire range of human attributes can be classified in the following categories:

a) Essential

b) Desirable

c) Optional

Essential may in fact be referred to the Star qualities which are required to be present in a candidate for undertaking and launching any career. You can't expect success or positive results if you are found lacking in them. Desirable qualities are those which may be present at the time of starting the career but not considered so essential because they do not serve any purpose at the beginning of the career. But, as you proceed in your service and look for promotions and progressive success in your performance, you realise the need and importance of these desirable qualities which then shift to consideration of essential category. You start feeling their further need as they influence your performance and demonstrate their effectiveness to your superiors for achieving significant results at advanced stages of your service period. Besides, these desirable qualities become Star Plus because of their specific importance to a particular career or service like Defence, Paramilitary services, Central / State class One / Two services. Optional class of qualities makes normally no difference in general even if they are present or absent but they become significant and are essentially required for those who wish to achieve high ranks and top positions in any service or industry.

Promotional Aspect

Against this background of classification, if you closely examine the list of attributes of both positive and negative types as given in the Annexure 1 of Chapter 2, it reveals that they have intrinsic relationship with the human nature, character, talent and personality. The proportion of their presence varies from the lowest level or none to the maximum marking level of 9. It is not necessary that all of them should be present in you but there is no denying the fact that it is desirable that you should possess positive attributes to the maximum extent possible and negative attributes to the least extent possible.

For undertaking any specific career or project or service or course, certain positive attributes which are called Star Plus qualities are invariably required besides normal the Star qualities but their need and level vary according to different types of careers and services. As promotional prospects occur and their possibility enhances in the service period of an individual, it is observed that the need for possession of additional positive attributes increases in number and proportion and those of the negative attributes proportionately reduces to lower levels. For reaching higher or near top positions in a particular branch of career or service, you have to possess largest number of positive attributes which enable you to lead and shoulder higher responsibilities of higher appointments that a particular organisation offers to you by virtue of your proven track record in performance and remarkable contribution to its interest.

Role of Upbringing and Education

It is stated that a boy or a girl when exposed to proper and systematic upbringing and given proper and extensive education develops positive qualities as listed in the Annexure 1 of Chapter 2. His success in life in his fields should therefore depend upon the type and quality of education and guidance he receives from the qualified and competent persons. It is also believed that proper and good upbringing, education and training produce good and powerful leaders, executives and bureaucrats for organising, managing and administrative purposes in any organisation, institute or industry.

The environment of upbringing and facilities of education offer excellent opportunities to you. The fact is that they are not available to all sections of the people especially those coming from the rural areas and having rural background. It results in causing a mental handicap in their growth. At the same time, it establishes fairly high opportunity level for those coming from the urban areas and environment where these facilities are easily available. Despite the fact that such an opportunity is available equally to a large number of candidates, it is generally observed that only a few of them perform well in their careers and a very few of them who can be counted on fingertips achieve senior and higher positions and reach top positions from this lot. It is because they possess different receptivity, grasping power, responsiveness, will power and proactive approach to such type of intensive education and training. They also possess different potential, ability, spontaneity and assimilation capacity to convert such facilities into positive action and fruitful results

It is therefore observed that this aspect has definitely got a bearing and correlation to the personal attributes. Accordingly, they are influenced and proportionately produce the end result. It however remains one of the domineering and determining factors in causing influence on destiny of an individual. The belief that proper upbringing and education are essential does not necessarily hold good in practice when it is seen that many such persons are facing failure or not making any grade or have left midway in career despite have received good education and training. It however remains a desirable and highly effective factor for influencing the career prospects of individuals.

It is now proposed to discuss the objective of this chapter in the subsequent paragraphs.

Approach

Considering the unique and differential aspects of human nature as observed in the wide range of personal attributes varying over a wide spectrum in numbers and proportions, it is necessary to examine their need based aspect for different types of careers and services. Besides, there is a question whether it is sufficient to have these personal attributes or there is any additional requirement over and above them when you have to select and decide about a particular career or service. It is already emphasised that there is a need to have maximum positive attributes and minimum negative attributes in a candidate for giving good performance and avoiding loss or failure in his career. There are certain additional factors to be considered before you make the final selection about the best and most suitable career from the lot available at a particular time. Before efforts are made to identify those additional factors for your guidance and assistance in selection of a proper career or course or profession or service, let us identify the users for this aspect as under:-

a) Students at the level of higher secondary examination
b) Students at the graduate level
c) Candidates who are already graduate or postgraduate and in temporary employment but look and try to seek a proper career or course of their choice and interest.

Student Level

Choice of a particular career or course which has to be made at the stage of 10 + 2 examination or graduate level is a crucial and critical factor for any student as it gives direction to his future prospects. It is generally found that students have very little understanding and awareness about their own personal attributes including basic Star qualities. They should therefore carry out proper analysis about their own qualities by adopting the process of Introspection and find out their strong as well as weak points.

SWAIT Analysis for Self-Appraisal

An analysis which is adopted for introspection or self-assessment is referred in management parlance as SWOT. It has been modified to include two additional factors A and I, drop O as Opportunities and combine it with T as Time. Such a modified acronym is called SWAIT. Its meaning and clarification are given as under:

a) **S** – Stands for Strengths which indicate strong points of your nature, character and personality and are shown in the form of having positive attributes. In other words, find out your Star and Star Plus qualities.

b) **W**—Stands for Weaknesses which indicate weak points of your nature, character and personality. They are manifested in the form of your negative attributes such as those referred as Negative Star qualities.

c) **A**—Stands for Aptitude which refers to your talent, capacity, urge and willingness to learn. It implies your mental adaptability and comprehension for suitably selecting, following and achieving success with your total involvement in it.

d) **I**— Stands for Interest. It means your preferred activity which implies your determination, creativity, initiative and dedication in order to follow and sustain for a long period of time.

e) **T**—Stands for Threats to yourself like your fear, apprehension, bias financial difficulties, competition. It also includes timing for availing opportunities as different careers and courses take different time span for completion and maturity. Events like competition, employment prospects, market situation, operating environment are time dependent and therefore related to offering opportunities at right time. Hence, course duration and its completion becomes an important factor for consideration.

Students who seek proper and suitable career or service should carry out their SWAIT Analysis honestly, sincerely, conscientiously and truthfully and assess its results before they proceed for seeking guidance and counseling from a competent person.

IQ

IQ means Intelligence Quotient. It is the modern means to know one's level of intelligence. The people are generally found interested to know about their personality, temperament, intelligence, traits, abilities and complexes.

It is basically a psychological concept and mainly pertains to mental abilities and functions. It therefore leads to your mental process of understanding, judgement, response, comprehension, assimilation and reasoning of any issue or problem. It also becomes a measure of your talent. It plays very important role in your education, upbringing and learning of professional skills in training courses. A student who scores higher marks or achieve merit in an examination is said to have high IQ compared to another student, having simple first or second class in the same examination.

IQ is one of the aspects of Star and Star Plus attributes, pertaining mainly to intelligence factor. It thus becomes one of the important determining factors for career selection and promotion in service. It is however advised that IQ of a candidate should be assessed in the field of his interest and choice where their mental faculties work efficiently and effectively. Judgement in academic sphere alone is likely to mislead you. You should therefore be cautious while universally using these criteria.

Academic Performance

For most of the students, especially coming from rural areas and who could not afford to have proper teaching in good reputed schools or expensive public schools, their performance in the final higher secondary examination becomes the realistic indicator of their capabilities and potentialities. Academic excellence despite rural background and drawbacks reveals a lot about their high level of mental robustness and intelligence (IQ) as well as aptitude and high caliber for taking any career or course. Such type of students, having excellent academic performance give us an indirect indicator of possessing star attributes with high level of intelligence. Unfortunately, they may not be aware of their own Self as it is likely to get shadowed by the rural conditions and family background.

What is therefore needed for them at this juncture is proper guidance and direction with financial support if required. At times, it is their ambition and willpower that motivate and drive these students to look around, search and seek proper advice and guidance. If these students carry out self-assessment and self-appraisal properly and systematically according to the guidelines given as above, it will become much easier for them to perceive the need and source for proper career guidance and selection.

Exposure to Public Schooling

Parents do make anxious and strenuous efforts to put their children in the best available and affordable schools for education up to higher secondary level. This is the initial and formative phase of education for the child. Keeping certain specific advantages in mind, although such public schooling costs heavily and drains out substantial financial resources of the parents, a child gets wide exposure in educational and extracurricular activities and a chance to develop his personality, individuality and identity on the wider fronts of knowledge, leadership, public relations, articulation, manners, vision, competitive spirit and confidence.

Having gone through such a public schooling successfully and achieved fairly good results in the progressive and final examination, the child is definitely placed at a higher threshold and comparatively advantageous position for seeking proper opening with bright prospects in areas of status, rank, fame, grade, fortune and prosperity. The child must remain conscious and aware of this fact which should always drive and motivate him to search and get career related information generally available from the city book shops and seek proper career guidance from the competent and knowledgeable persons. He should have inquisitive mind, pragmatic approach and specific purpose for his future course of action. As a child is about to complete schooling after giving final examination, he should ask the following pertinent questions to himself for remaining motivated to search and seek proper career:

a) What was the purpose of your parents in putting you in a public school of expensive nature?
b) Were you able to develop your specific qualities such as work style, manners, expression, communication skill, relationship, leadership, knowledge and so on?
c) What are your specific developments and achievements during the course of public schooling?
d) What level of confidence, have you now got about your individuality, personality, intelligence, aptitude and will power in order to achieve your end objective in life?

CAREERS AND COURSES

Different types of careers and courses which are available to students for selection and which need intensive type of SWAIT Analysis as described above are given in the various fields as under:

a) Engineering, Computer Sciences and Technical services.
b) Medical, Health and Life Sciences and Services.
c) Administrative, Foreign, Revenue and Forest Services at both central and state government levels such as IAS,IFS, IRS and so on.
d) Defence Services such as Army, Navy and Air Force.
e) Police and Paramilitary Forces such as CRPF, BSF, ISF, CBI, and so on.
f) Commercial and Financial Services such as Cost, Charter Accountancy Custom, Tax, Excise and so on.
g) Business Management such as Sales, Marketing, Financing
h) Utility Services such as Hotel, Secretarial, Fashion, Textile, Tourism and so on.
i) Transport Services such as Surface, Water, Aviation and Marine
j) Teaching and Academic Services such as teaching in schools, colleges, institutions, academies, university and doing research and development activities in laboratories of Industrial and Scientific Council, Defence and Agricultural Organisations.
k) Vocational courses such as Fine Arts, Music, Painting, Dance, Acting, Modelling
l) Self-employment Services such as Manufacturing, Trading, Transport, Consultancy, Repairing, Servicing, etc
m) Construction, Real Estate, Broker Agency
n) Journalism, Anchoring TV Shows.
o) Judiciary and Legal Services
p) Sport and Games for participation, training and administration.

SELECTION MODE

It is generally found that students after completion of their 10 + 2 or graduate courses approach their teachers and other local known experienced persons in order to seek guidance and advice for selection of a suitable course or career for them. Before they approach, it is emphasized that the students must be serious, honest and willing for seeking career advice. They must carry out their SWAIT Analysis and self-assessment in order to ascertain their abilities, personal specific qualities and aptitude. In order to guide them in their efforts to seek proper advice, they must do serious and honest homework as stated above and prepare a guide sheet, containing answers to the following suggestive questions:

a) Did you carry out Introspection and Self-Assessment about your personal attributes of both positive and negative types as given in Annexure 1 of Chapter 2?
b) If so, did you identify your star and star plus as well as negative star qualities and mark them separately for your sincere and serious consideration?
c) Did you carry out SWAIT analysis for yourself?
d) If so, did you identify strong and weak points of your nature, character and personality?
e) Do you have specific likes and dislikes for any career or service or profession?
f) Are you aware and conscious about your aptitude or liking for independent working in Administrative or Investigative or Law Enforcing Branches?
g) Have you skill and flair for writing or oratory and working with team spirit.
h) Have you marked your ultimate objective for achievement in life? It may be called life expectation or life aspiration such as wealth and fortune, fame and reputation, academic pursuit for knowledge and learning, owning business empire, adventure and leadership, social and welfare service, command and control position, creative art and related faculties like music, acting, painting and so on.

Parameters for Selection of Right Career

Having seen the selection mode and availability of various careers, you should ascertain and decide about your expectations from such a career / course. It is natural that after completion of the secondary schooling or college education, students have some notions and expectations about their future from the type of schooling or college education they received. While they wish and plan to select a particular career / course, they have valid question to ask as to why they should select this career and what benefits are likely to be available to them? Does it fit into their notional framework of mind as envisaged while in the school or college ?

This type of situation exists even when you look for a particular job. You would have certain valid expectations from such a job. You should have kept them in mind while searching for it. In fact, you have to think about what you want from such a career / job or whether it is capable of offering things which you look for. The list of the benefits which you may have in your mind is given as under:

a) **Financial Security**—Does the career offer you enough money to enjoy the life style you want?

b) **Autonomy**—Availability of freedom to do what you like to do and be independent.

c) **Managing People**—Possibility to deal with organisational H.R. policies and have delegated powers.

d) **Responsibility**—Possibility of making other people responsible for their jobs just as making yourself responsible and accountable for your performance.

e) **Achievement and Creativity** --Availability of scope to make a contribution which is special, novel and challenging.

f) **Self-Esteem and Recognition**—Ability to have a feeling that you are somebody with self respect and should be respected by others. Also scope to receive rewards and acclaim for your creative works and performance.

g) **Social Contact**—Scope for working and developing relationship with others.

h) **Work Flexibility**—Scope to change the duties and jobs for career diversification and internal movement for performing different in -house jobs.

I) **Outdoor Activities**—Whether scope for movements outside for outdoor jobs such as marketing and sale activities is viable?

j) **Personal Growth, Development and Status**—Opportunities and scope for developing your personal potential and promotions to higher ranks.
k) **Risks and Challenges**—Opportunities to face risks and challenges and show results with your leadership qualities.
l) **Work/Leisure Balance**—Whether career / job can offer you enough time for your leisure and family?

Now, you have to really ask yourself what is really important from a particular career, having wide scope for offering opportunities, capabilities and work culture. You should remember these different aspects of any career while searching and selecting one from a lot. Your Self-Assessment and Self-Appraisal will definitely play a dominant role in this process

Interest Areas

It is observed that life expectation or life aspiration aspect as well as aptitude has got indirect relation and bearing on your personal attributes which enable you to directly address and finally assess your abilities and characteristics of your nature and personality. Since personal liking factor plays an important role in selection and growth of a career and course, it is felt pertinent to specifically address this issue and assist you for seeking pointed answers to the following questions related to your interest areas:

a) If you have interest in knowing why and how things work as well as how things are constructed or produced, then your related interest area is Engineering, Technical and Physical sciences.
b) If you take interest in knowing why and how leaving creatures including human beings work and how diseases occur and what their cure are, then your related interest areas are Health, Life and Medical Sciences.
c) If you love to interact and work with people for your gain, your related field is in Management of trade, Sales and Marketing.
d) If you like to systematically work as per rules and procedures, exercise power and position over public, keep proper records, then your related field is Finance / Accounts / Auditing / Administration.
e) If you like the rule of law and order, discipline, criminal investigation and respect for law, then your related interest lies in Police and Paramilitary Forces.

f) If you like adventure, challenges, leadership, games, handling of weapons and sacrifice for the nation, then your field is Defence Forces.

g) If you enjoy serving people and look for only sustainable return, then your career is Social Services.

h) If art, music, painting, interior design, modeling, acting interest you then your interest field is Vocational.

i) If you like self control, self reliance and independent working and own freedom of action then you better go for your own profession, job and enterprise.

j) If you like teaching, writing, preaching and guiding in pursuit of knowledge then your field is Academic, Literature and Teaching profession.

The interest areas as indicated above are stated on sample basis. You should also bear in mind that physical body standards and IQ. Levels merit important consideration for different occupations and services as they demand different physical and mental requirements and standards like Defence and Paramilitary Forces, Research Institutions, etc.

You are now in a position to write your detailed Self-Appraisal Report strictly according to SWAIT Analysis and guidelines given as above. The format for writing this report is given along with certain introspective questions in the Annexure ? to this chapter. With homework, your position becomes definitely much better and realistic to seek proper, positive, meaningful and productive guidance and advice for your career and courses from competent teachers and knowledgeable experienced persons.

Guidance and Counselling

Whenever students or candidates who are concerned for their careers or services approach you for consultation and advice on career related subjects, you assume the important and responsible role of an Advisor. You therefore need to be really careful, cautious and honest in giving your advice in areas of their interests and your expertise only. It will be absolutely honourable say NO if you do not know or have very limited information on the subject. Nevertheless, you should be tactful and forceful inquire if a student has already done his homework of Self-

Assessment and prepared Self-Appraisal Report like SWAIT Analysis and if the answer is YES, then you should proceed to initiate your advisory action on the following lines:

a) Check the homework done by the student and verify if it is properly and systematically done in order to ascertain his seriousness and involvement. This homework may be in the form Self-Appraisal Report.

b) Study and analyse the homework and assess his important aspects such as abilities, characteristics, aptitude, interest areas, potential, mindset and so on.

c) Ascertain about his life expectation or aspiration and ask him what he wants to become and what is his ambition for rising and achieving high level posts and ranks in that particular career field.

d) Encourage students to ask questions or seek clarifications on any issue of their interest.

e) Suggest at least two careers or courses, one essential and another optional from the indicative list already given above. While advising on this issue, you should be aware about their prospects and growth potential and ascertain from a student if such a career or course in his opinion suits his life aspirations.

Guidelines for Career Advice

It is observed that students who approach you for advice belong to different categories such as those who have passed their higher secondary examination or those who have done their graduation and are looking for joining proper career / course / service. Vast field of different types of careers and courses that are today available has been stated above in a comprehensive manner. Now, let us take a look at various types of students who have completed their education at different levels and types of careers and courses which should suit them commensurate to the basic qualifications which they have achieved from different types of education as given below.:

a) **For students who have passed their 12th standard examination:** The courses which are suitable for such students are mostly professional for giving hand working skills and supervisory abilities at diploma level on actual working platform like industry, hospital, hotel, and so on. It offers an opportunity to join Defence and Paramilitary Forces as a soldier or National Defence Academy (NDA) on the basis of competitive examination for subsequently attaining officer's grade in Army, Navy and Air Force. It also enables you to join professional courses such as Engineering, Medical, Agriculture and Veterinary courses in order to gain a professional degree and subsequently specialised qualifications.

b) **For students after becoming graduates in Science, Commerce and Art:** It enables you to appear for state and national level competitive examinations conducted by the state public and union public service commissions whereby you have a chance to directly gain officer's grade at class 2 or class 1 level. It enables you to join state level services in various branches like police, taxation, revenue, excise and so on. Banking, Railway, Forestry, Judiciary and other utility services demand graduate level candidates as working and supervisory staff. It opens out a field to pursue an independent profession, trade, enterprise business or small scale manufacturing unit.

c) **For students after gaining degree in Engineering and Medical Services:** You can join government / private services. You can also do post graduation and specialisation in specific subjects, discipline and areas. You can appear for central government services through UPSC examination after full preparation and coaching. You can appear before the Service Selection Board of the Army, Navy and Air Force in order to get commissioned officer's rank in their technical and medical branches with special benefits in rank and seniority. You can enter the academic field for teaching and doing scientific research and development works after post graduation.

There are books available in the market on career guidance and selection which give the list of courses and addresses of institutions which are running them all over the country. Details of course duration, qualifications and employment potential are given in them for general information of the public. It is advisable to refer the updated books for guidance.

Ethics for Advisors

It has already been pointed out that the person whose advice is sought by a student should be honest to admit their limitations about the knowledge and information which should actually pertain to the interest areas of the students. You should take an approach and reference of the students to you seriously and patiently. You should therefore fully devote your attention and time to them. You can always ask a student to approach you later at the time of your convenience if your present time and engagement are not permitting your proper devotion. Meanwhile, you can study and analyse the homework if done or ask to do it as per the guidelines given here if not done and then ask the student to approach you later with prior appointment. Aim of this exercise is to take career advising task seriously, sincerely and honestly by both parties with proper prior homework work done in the form of Self-Appraisal Report. Such an approach is necessary to produce positive and meaningful results as it has longtime repercussions over his life as he is now making a beginning in life and anxiously looking for support and guidance from elderly knowledgeable persons.

Independent Approach

It is possible that you may not get proper, knowledgeable and competent person or advisor especially in the fields and areas which you wish to select from central or state level administrative services as career at class 1 or class 2 levels. You should be aware that there is a tough and stiff competition and you have to rigorously go through the mandatory written examinations and oral interviews at different times. These examinations need collection of wide information, intensive hard work, extensive studies and in-depth preparation. For this purpose, you have got to have strong motivation, urge, will power, patience and total dedication along with outside support for periodic guidance and financing.

Hence, it is essential that you should seriously and sincerely carry out your Self-Assessment and SWAIT Analysis and then come to the conclusion about your real potential, capacity, capability, aptitude, talent and availability of support from outside sources. Your performance in annual examinations at graduate and other initial competitive levels gives an indication about your intellectual level and intrinsic potential.

Besides, it calls for patience, perseverance, mission oriented approach and strong willpower to pursue the goal to its logical conclusion even when involving a number of attempts, if success is denied to you at the first qualifying attempt. Under these circumstances, you should review the process and the result of your self-assessment and self-appraisal for identifying those factors which need special attention and emphasis for intensifying your efforts, drive and pursuit.

If the result of your self-assessment and self-appraisal is strongly assertive and positive, then proceed and pursue it by all means. You will be armed with proper justification about your selection and pursuit which will be appreciated and you will get outside support and encouragement without any hesitation and doubt. On the other hand, if you have not properly carried out your home work and still wish to pursue such high level competitive careers on the basis of your confidence, intuition, gut feelings and judgement, you are taking a serious risk in your career and shooting an arrow in the darkness for success. Your optimistic approach to believe that you will eventually succeed on account of your intensive hard work and progressive build up of confidence at the preparation level is appreciated, but it carries a high risk with probability of 50 percent success. Under this situation, you are advised to keep your other options open to avail after closing of chances in the competitive examinations. It should however be noted that you are now placed in a much better position because of your exposure and preparation on a wide front and your chances for attempting other services become brighter. But, the price already paid by you in the form of loss of valuable time, opportunities and financial costs remains of prime concern and consideration, having longtime repercussions on your life which are perhaps not possible to foresee at this stage.

Preparation for the competitive examinations takes a normal time period of two to three years and perhaps more if additional attempts are involved. During this period, you need continuous moral and financial support for capital expenses involving purchase of books, library facilities and sustenance of your living and morale. As such, a candidate should do proper planning and organise means to ensure procurement of adequate and timely financial support from outside sources in case family support is not available. In this respect, good academic performance and positive results of your self-assessment and self-appraisal become quite handy and comes to your help in order to convince and achieve such support from your family members or outside resources.

Decision-Making Process

By now, you have carried out your self-assessment and self-appraisal with SWAIT Analysis. You have also examined your interest areas and various career and courses which are easily available and should suit your capabilities and resources. You have also contacted competent and knowledgeable person and sought his proper and meaningful advice and counseling. Thus, you have come to a stage for taking decision of your own.

Decision making or taking is a very important, crucial and strenuous process, involving risk and far reaching future consequences in your life. Hence, every caution, prudence and judicious approach must be adopted and exercised after considering all the pros and cons before finally selecting the right career or course which should meet your life expectation as envisaged by you for your own future.

Decision making implies choice from several possibilities which open many courses of action before you. Each one offers its own pros and cons along with benefits and cost liabilities. In order to guide and effectively assist you in this respect, a plan of five points is suggested as under:

a) **Define your objective.** Specify the aim or objectives which you wish to achieve on short as well as long term basis.

b) **Collect adequate information:** Collect information about various careers / courses. Organise it and seek advice and clarifications. Check facts and opinions and identify possible and achievable options.

c) **Develop options and alternatives:** List possible courses for action within your means and support. Select the one which could be achievable within the time frame, dictated by your family and background conditions.

d) **Evaluate and decide:** List out pros and cons and their consequences. Anticipate risks and road blocks and continuous support from within and outside sources.

e) **Implement:** Act to carry out the decision so arrived. Keep monitoring and reviewing from time to time.

The steps stated as above are involved in any rational and systematic decision making process. It implies cautious, careful and risk free approach. It is needless to say that it is time and effort consuming and likely to cause some delay in reaching the final conclusion. Since the stakes of the individual or organisation involved in this process are high with long-term repercussions, it is not advisable to sacrifice systematic and rational approach in arriving at the right decision. Hence, appropriate time should be given to the process.

At our stage, the scope of decision is limited to selection of the right career / course which should meet the parameters as stated above. As such, the process is simplified and it is easily feasible for an individual to adopt and take decision as under:

a) Instantly based on his intuition or instinct.
b) After giving careful thought over the material presented before you.
c) After consultation with senior persons who are experienced, knowledgeable and belong to different streams.
d) After listening to arguments from both sides and reading in between the lines through one's mental reasoning and judgement.

The person who follows the proper process and procedure as stated above in (b), (c) and (d) is placed in a better position to take correct and precise decision. Although the decision under (a) is generally appreciated and becomes indicator of one's decisive nature, it sometimes happens to be autocratic, authoritative and irrational and may prove risky and counter productive. You should therefore exercise your option carefully, prudently and judiciously and take the decision for yourself accordingly.

The Career Game

While concluding this chapter, it is pointed out that your career is really a game which has specific and definite rules and procedures for playing with the ultimate objective to win it. While making career choices, you are in a way choosing your playing field, teammates, the rules and regulations by which you will play with the goal lines and your opponents. Playing field determines the environment, surrounding and work place for your career to operate. Teammates determine the types of personnel; you will be working with their background, experience and knowledge which matter to form a team. Teammates will play supportive as well as competitor's role. Some teammates will be traditional and some spontaneous and progressive type. Rules and regulations are designed to expedite work functions and protect it from outside forces. Goal lines are seen as commonly agreed standards for success. This sets boundary limits, giving direction of push and kicking the goal. Opponents signify the competitive field and will be working to oppose your objective that is to win.

Now, the question is how you look at the career game. Firstly, choose a game that allows you to fully express your purpose. Choose a career such that you want to do something explicitly to meet your life aspirations. Secondly, choose a game that allows you to fully express your talents and abilities. Thirdly, choose a game that is compatible with your personality. Finally, choose a game to which you can commit yourself. In other words, you can get into a game and remain there for excelling. You should also feel respect and sense of honour in playing the game.

Finally, the game of your life's career and work should have personal affirmations in the form of commitments for guidance and progress. These should come in the forms as under:

a) Expression of your lifelong work.

b) Playing the game with intensity without being too serious.

c) Have energy, will, and persistence to face and find information

d) Be totally honest and realistic in your self-appraisal.

e) Be optimistic and confident for rising and achieving success in your career.

f) Trust yourself with full conviction.

g) Be determined and remain committed for achieving your purpose with team spirit and self-motivation.

(See Annexure 2 for Self-assessment and Self-appraisal Report form).

4

Self-Improvement and Self-development

SCOPE

1. What are the external influencing factors?
2. How will you set your personal mission?
3. What are the leadership traits? How effective is their role in your service career?
4. What is the self-driven process for self-development?
5. What is the road map for your self-development?
6. How will you guard and avoid pitfalls in your career?
7. How will you evaluate success and failure in your life?
8. How will you console a person who has met failure?

Purpose

There are two aspects of human life. While one pertains to improvement in its existing structure and framework, the other concerns to create and establish development thereby giving a new look and appearance to the existing entity. Both are focused to cause in their own ways a change in their existing static situation. As you know, static life is quite dull, monotonous and causes weariness, mental fatigue and retardation. In fact, change is an essential part of the natural process. It is seen everywhere in the nature and its weather, climate, temperature, seasons, etc. That is how the human life has become exciting, thrilling, interesting and therefore worth living. So, whenever you set in the process of change, you move forward in the direction of progress thereby taking you to a high stature, position, status. Your living style and standards are enriched to a highly comfortable level. Now, the question is how to do it and what is the process and what entities are to be handled.

Incidentally, while deliberating on the destiny and its correlation with personal attributes, you are not supposed to get discouraged and cease your efforts for achieving self-development. In fact, you are able to see a clear path and the efforts required for you to successfully achieve your objective Thus, you get ample scope for taking appropriate steps for correction and improvement after carrying out the introspective process. While doing so, you come to know the intimate relationship and interactive influence of exterior forces on your attributes and the end result accruing thereoff. In this process, you remain a key figure and main actor for causing improvement and initiation of self-development related process and action. Your personal role which is entirely related to your personal attributes' profile, skill and abilities is crucial and remains pioneering. Thus, it will not be prudent and wise to pass on blame to others and external circumstances for your failure or loss of opportunities as and when it occur in your life. By now, you know that your nature, character, talent, mindset, performance depend upon your personal qualities of both positive and negative types. They also affect your career and achievement of its objectives. So, let us examine the influence of various external factors on your career aspect and the role of your personal qualities in causing its development under certain specific circumstances.

PARENTS' INFLUENCE

Parents have the vital role to play in influencing and guiding the destiny of their wards. They always feel that their wards are obliged to follow their wishes. While their right is not denied in this respect, they should adopt an amicable, pragmatic, cooperative and tolerant approach and be reasonable and sympathetic to their ward's wishes, likes and interest areas. Today, parents should avoid coercive, autocratic and assertive approach and establish a two way communication channel with their wards in order to know their mind and trends. In this respect, the following guidelines are recommended for parents:

a) Find out the strong and weak attributes of your wards. Examine closely their nature, habits, behaviour, conduct and attitude. Keep the record of their abnormal behaviour, impulsive response and peculiar habits.

b) Update yourself by gaining knowledge and information about various career and courses that are available and their utilities and service potential.

c) Discuss freely and frankly with your wards and members of the family about the information which have gained as above and also other issues which you find useful for their careers.

d) Always try to find time to sit and talk to your children and patiently listen to their views. Watch their reaction to your advice. Also keep a watch on their friends, their behaviour and habits.

e) Estimate your resources to support your wards till completion of their education and end of financial dependence in all respects. Offer your resources and support voluntarily and without any hitch.

f) Adopt the technique for instilling the following factors in your wards:

   i) Will power, vision and motivation.

   ii) Confidence, foresight and forethought.

   iii) Concentration and responsiveness.

   iv) Self-discipline, code of conduct and values.

   v) Urge for excellent performance in studies and academics.

g) Avoid sarcastic remarks and frequent ticking off.

h) Act like a catalyst in fostering the self-development process of your wards.

While following this path, it is also the duty of a ward to listen to the views and advice of his parents and believe that their advice is for his best interest and welfare. The following guidelines are stated for the wards to follow:

a) Treat your parents as your best friend, guide and well wisher.

b) Listen to their advice patiently and appreciate the element of affection, attachment, concern and honesty in their advice.

c) Talk and discuss with them frankly, freely and logically without fear and appraise them about modern developments around and challenges to be faced.

d) Avoid confrontation and heated arguments with your parents and be calm and patient while listening to them.

e) Try to demonstrate your progress and positive points to your parents in order to change their mind to your way of thinking and interest.

It is finally pointed out that it is a two-way communicative dialogue. The respect and mutual understanding between the two will certainly help to find the best possible way out of any problem and issue.

Influence of Environment

Environment in this respect is described as rural or urban, backward or forward, literate or illiterate, poor or rich, social or antisocial, cooperative or uncooperative, polluted or unpolluted, silent or noisy and so on. Such an environment generates conducive and favorable conditions or has a reverse influence on proper upbringing and self-development. There are numerous examples where the individuals have come out from abject, adverse environment and still achieved fairly top positions of prosperity and reputation. It is however pointed out that this aspect does not become an impending and hindering factor in respect of those persons, having strength and power of their positive attributes which dominate in their academic and career activities for producing success at every stage of their activities. They no doubt are handicaps but the presence of their star plus attributes overcomes the effects of adverse environment and pull them up on the basis of their ambition, committed struggle, drive, determination and motivation. Some persons do get discouraged and handicapped but it is finally their strong positive attributes which cause development and determine their career advancement.

Studies and Academics

Your performance in studies and academics is largely influenced by your positive attributes such as hard work, dedication, intelligence and perseverance. Committed hard work, drive and will power are definitely required for your excellent or very good performance in your academics. In fact, sustained excellent performance in annual examinations has today become a pace setter in judgement and assessment for considering your suitability and fitness for further education and undertaking prestigious careers / services. It is pointed out that students, having excellent performance in their final examinations or faculties such as engineering, medical and commercial do not face much problems for employment in industries and other organisations because of the demonstration of star plus attributes as revealed in such candidates.

Habits vs Attributes

Every individual has got certain habits, some visible and some invisible. These habits have a direct impact on his nature and behaviour in private, office and public places. Habit is a way of behaviour in a set pattern. It occurs repetitively whenever it gets excited by an external impulse. Negative impression is generally formed about an individual when his peculiar habits cause embarrassment in public.

Habits and personal attributes have got close interactive relationship. Positive or negative habits occur in an individual from a complex mix of a few positive and negative attributes which result in causing prominent impact on behaviour in a specific way depending upon the dominant role being played by one of them at a time.

State of Mental Health

A lot of psychological studies have been done in this respect. A robust, healthy and strong mental state of a person is essential for his positive, amicable, sociable and inspiring nature, behaviour and personality. Mental health and mindset of an individual are closely related and influence his outlook and approach which eventually turn out to be positive or negative, forward or backward, pragmatic or orthodox.

It is pointed out that mental health has close relation with your personal attributes. Dominance of negative attributes in your nature such as anger, hot temper, ego, envy, aggressiveness will make you mentally sick, tired and retarded thereby making you unhappy, sullen and disappointed. On the other hand, dominance of positive attributes will make you feel inspired, contended and happy and bring out the positive, pragmatic and constructive factor in your outlook and nature. Hence, positive attributes in either dominant or balanced form are essentially required in order to maintain a healthy mental state.

Influence of Yoga / Meditation

Yoga and meditation are today recognised as one of the most important means for self-development and discipline. Students are advised to do yoga and meditation regularly after completion of strenuous study in a day. It trains your mind to concentrate and initiate the positive thinking process on specific issues thereby giving exercise and relaxation to your faculties and senses. A regular practice of yoga and meditation helps you to improve your thinking power and memory which result in your balanced, quiet and positive outlook. Besides, it offers you a healthy mind and body which enable you to concentrate on studies and keep you away from wild and stray thoughts.

In this respect, you are advised to go for a long walk after completing your studies for the day. Thus, you not only exercise your body but also get an opportunity to recollect, think and analyze what you have read and studied during the day and plan your future course.

Setting of Personal Mission

This is the first most important step in the direction of your self- development. Whenever you take up a career or course, you must have specific objective in your mind which drives you to pursue and accomplish it. If you are not able to define and express your objective in your mission, your approach remains casual, ambiguous and uncertain with no concentration and economic utilization of resources, time and efforts.

In this respect, the author has interacted and talked to a number of students of engineering and other courses and tried to ascertain their objectives and future plans. Some just shrugged their shoulders and were vague. Some could pin their hopes just on getting low level jobs after completing the prestigious courses. They did not even show interest in knowing the prospects and market potentials of their courses.

Hence, setting an objective for achievement with all your possible efforts should be the first and foremost part of your mission. In this respect, your following attributes become quite visible and effective:

a) Vision and will power.

b) Drive and motivation.

c) Persistent hard work and a positive mindset

d) Concentration of efforts and resources.

e) Systematic approach and planning by setting a road map with distinct milestones for achieving progress

f) Commitment and firm determination

g) Intelligence and maturity.

This process of personal mission should be based on proper planning and complete information, pertaining to a particular career or course. It should be a deliberate and well thought process and involve consultation and discussion with knowledgeable and well-informed persons. You must have a set of intelligent and investigative questions in your mind, aimed at finding extensive information about the course potential with promotional avenues to higher levels. You should then fix your bearing in a particular direction and set the mission objective fairly high with specific milestones for achievement stepwise and reviewing progress. The objective so set should be reachable with your talent, efforts and resources at your disposal. It is always advisable to set a high objective and you should then try to achieve it as much as possible. In this way, one should feel contended and pleased on the progress gained but always leave scope for putting further efforts and resources in order to reach your ultimate destination.

You must avoid frustration and disappointment in case you fail to achieve your set mission objective so long as you are convinced about putting your sincere and honest efforts according to a well thought action plan. Certain individuals do not wish to set an objective and wish to adopt a watch and wait approach in order to possibly avoid the frustration and disappointment of failure.

Self-driven Guidance

It should be noted that you are an entity of independent existence with individualistic features, attributes and mindset. You have complete command and control on yourself. As such, you are entirely and exclusively responsible for yourself in your life.

You are not aware about your abilities, potential and capabilities during the early period of youth. You are so much wrapped under care and attention of your parents and elders that you hardly get time to look at yourself. Of course, you do not have proper sense and understanding for judgment about yourself but you start demonstrating some of your attributes during the early period of your youth at various stages in the form of your performance and behaviour while undergoing primary and middle-level schooling. Although, it is too early to judge, parents should be careful and cautious at this stage in observing and assessing performance of their wards. They should arrange proper facilities in order to encourage the children to come up and show their attributes in one form or other like intellect, memory, awareness, willingness, responsiveness, enthusiasm, keenness, drive and so on.

It is observed that some children act on their own and decide to set the personal objective in their life. They may not be so expressive or vocal about it but start demonstrating their approach, inclination and intention and initiate steps in that direction of their own. At this stage, the only visible indicator of their mission and presence of positive star attributes is seen in their excellent performance in academics and examinations and at times from their conduct and expression of both facial and vocal types. Parents should carefully watch and observe this phase and offer support and proper encouragement to them.

Although, such wards are quite capable of their own in guiding themselves, they do look for proper guidance and advice from outside sources. It is in fact their spirit of self-drive and motivation which keep them prompting to seek outside advice and support without anybody telling them to do so. Such self driven and motivated students have a much better chance to do well and achieve excellent performance in their mission. They demonstrate promising prospects for self-development for achieving success in any job, career, course of any organisation and industry in which they can prove to be an asset and substantial contributor.

Leadership Traits

It is well known that there is need of a guiding hand in every human activity, involving a group of people. The head of a family is known as leader at the lowest level. Progress and fortune of a family depend upon the quality and effectiveness of its leader. Leaders are required at junior, middle, senior and higher levels in all walks of life but their responsibilities vary according to their functional levels.

The primary role of a leader is to achieve the task with available manpower and resources placed at disposal. A leader has to build a cohesive and harmonious team or group and lead it boldly, purposefully, intelligently and devotedly to achieve the end objective. He plays the leading role which covers the following activities:

a) Planning to achieve the goal.

b) Delegate the responsibilities by assigning work and resources.

c) Control and monitor the work and its progress.

d) Support by encouraging, motivating and training.

e) Evaluate the result on the basis of its cost and benefit.

A good and an effective leader should have the following attributes:

a) Honesty, knowledge, initiative and truthfulness.

b) Sense of duty, obligation, responsibility, accountability and morality.

c) Awareness about own shortcoming and limitation as well as strong points.

d) Respectfulness, selflessness, helpfulness and consciousness.

e) Commitment and dedication to the assigned mission objective.

f) Will power, drive, vision and determination.

g) Loyalty, enterprising spirit and decision taking ability

h) Communicative skill, tolerance and adaptability.

i) Handling people and relationship.

j) Control over temper and expression.

It will be seen that leadership traits are basically positive star and star plus attributes and their dominance over negative attributes establishes leading role of an individual in any service / business/ industry. There is a sense in saying that a leader is born in that it is your personal inborn attributes which play dominant role in shaping your personality and performance. Once, you perceive presence of such attributes in you, it is then possible to develop them by adopting an intensive training programme so as to enable you to become a big leader from a small leader in any organization, business group or industry. So, this is another way of self-development in the field of leadership

Self-Improvement and Development Process

While doing your self assessment and self appraisal, you come to know about the strong and weak points of your nature, behaviour and personality. You perform this exercise in an honest and sincere manner with a unique purpose "to know about yourself in depth". By now, you know what positive attributes should be encouraged for development and which negative attributes should be marked for control and remedial measures in order to avoid their negative impact and influence. Since you alone can exercise command and control on yourself and no body else, it is within your power, capacity and scope to develop and nourish some important attributes in order to get positive results in your life. It is however emphasized that there are certain positive factors present within you as inherent attributes which would drive and motivate you instinctively to adopt such measures for your self development. They are highlighted as under:

a) Adaptability
b) Responsiveness
c) Assimilation
d) Accommodativeness
e) Conscientiousness
f) Tolerance and patience
g) Open-mindedness
h) Diligence
i) Initiative and awareness

It should be noted that these positive attributes can produce positive result and make your self development process effective and meaningful provided you have:

(a) Vision and ambition
(b) Strong will power
(c) Awareness
(d) Clarity in mission and approach
(e) Commitment and involvement
(f) Positive mindset.

Steps / Measures for Self-development

Major approach and steps which guide and drive you to initiate a real Self- Development Programme are already given above in clear terms as flagship bearers. Besides, there exists a road map of activities which appear trivial in nature but they are quite significant and effective for causing your self-improvement and development. Incidentally, these steps / measures are applicable for causing both self-improvement and development. You can easily and conveniently adopt them in your daily activities. These steps / measures are now enumerated below.

a) Be gentle, polite, humble and respectful while dealing and talking with others and especially elderly person.

b) Adopt a cheerful posture and keep a smile on your face while talking or discussing with others. Avoid seriousness and gravity in your facial expression and behaviour.

c) Keep your temper down and maintain a quiet, patient and flexible attitude and approach.

d) Follow some hobbies. Look up to the nature and sky and perceive the laws of nature, controlling the universe and its activities. Be eco-friendly.

e) Plan your routine and prioritize certain events time wise for action. Observe time schedule and manage your discussion accordingly.

f) Look after your health and maintain it well with proper and regular diet and exercise. Practise yoga and meditation for achieving focus and concentration.

g) Learn to appreciate the work of others and avoid direct criticism.

h) Always carry a sense of responsibility and accountability.

i) Remain committed to the cause with firm determination. Avoid fickleness and restlessness.

j) Develop the art of framing specific, precise and inquisitive questions in a proper and clear language without bias or prejudice. Ask these questions on proper occasions and to the concerned persons.

k) Develop the habit of reading books, news papers and magazines. Keep extracts of important information for reference.

l) Learn the art of patient listening and vocal expression with clarity, fluency, poise and proper pause.

m) Observe discipline, tactfulness and code of conduct while behaving and dealing with others.

n) Visit often a place of worship and offer your prayer by keeping specific purpose in your mind like health, knowledge, fortune, fame etc.

o) Keep your urge to learn and know continuously. Try to become a good professional and manager.

p) Go on a trip away from your place regularly with your family members or friends in order to get change from a routine and relaxation.

q) Seek others' confidence and respect by showing your keenness, involvement and devotion.

r) In case of doubt, consult and seek proper advice and then decide.

s) Try to know your well wishers, patrons or sympathisers and ascertain their opinion about yourself. Remain in touch with them by sending greetings, best wishes on their birth anniversaries.

t) Remain always willing to work hard and offer your help or assistance voluntarily at home or outside without anybody asking for it.

u) Develop competitive spirit and work accordingly. Appear in competitive examinations and interviews and verify your abilities and potential. You always reserve your right to join or reject the offer. Remember that you are shying away and escaping from reality if you are just avoiding it without any valid reason.

v) Remember in life that there are no favors and nothing is available free of cost. So, you must pay for it in some form or doing some service in return as favours as well as outside help cost money.

w) Participate in social events with team spirit and hard work for achieving the goal. Also participate in group discussion and maintain your initiative with logic, reasoning and knowledge with full control on your expression.

x) Before appearing for any interview, prepare extensively and thoroughly for it including information about the organization and its products and then answer questions with gentleness, confidence and maturity. Avoid bluffing and arguments and remain polite, humble and poised throughout the period of interview.

y) Express apology when you are wrong or inadvertently cause harm or inconvenience to others. Also express your thanks for any favour or help you receive.

z) Never say no bluntly and curtly even if you disagree. Remember that there are indirect ways of expressing your disapproval in a tactful and polite way and also your views with a smile on your face.

It is however pointed out that how much you are going to adopt, follow and practice will depend upon your nature and character. In other words, it means, ultimately, responses from your personal attributes of both positive and negative types. Development process is possible and gets in motion whenever favourable and conducive conditions exist for its growth to occur. As such, if there is a dominance of certain positive attributes over negative attributes, there definitely exists a scope for self-development. In that case, the results will be definitely encouraging and extremely useful when you follow the road map of guidance as given above.

As regards the education and upbringing factor as stated in Chapter 2, it certainly helps as an external means to assist the self-development process. Combined effect of both means is tremendously productive and emphatic in respect of achieving career promotions and advancement in any organisation and industry.

Watch and Guard for Avoiding Pitfalls

While you are involved in the process of adopting measures for self development and as you progressively comply with them, it is necessary for you to know those areas which are likely to cause adverse influence on you and result in failure despite your best and sincere efforts and intention. Any slippage or remaining ignorant about these areas will cost you heavily and reverse the process of your progress any time without your knowledge or you coming to know about it because its ill and adverse effects are not felt directly and instantly but produce slow cumulative damaging effect on your career.

If that is the case despite you having positive attributes to overcome them, it is better to watch and guard against those adverse vicious areas so that the energy and efforts from your positive attributes could be spent fruitfully and constructively elsewhere and at the same time, you avoid or minimise the chances of failure in your mission / task.

The list of such areas which are referred as pitfalls, having potential to cause failure in your personal career is given as under:

a) Spending more than you earn will never enable you to gain wealth.

b) Running into debt and temptation to adopt corrupt practices.

c) Scattering your resources, power and efforts on a wide front.

d) Losing sight and remaining unaware about your "brain" especially when you are required to be alert, active and agile to respond and react to adverse situation.

e) Blaming others thereby losing sight of your mistakes and slippages. as committed knowingly or unknowingly.

f) Indulging, recounting and clinging to the past in stead of concentrating on the present and proceeding forward.

g) Taking short cuts for getting quick and easy results and returns.

h) Neglecting and overlooking details in order to tie up loose ends.

i) Quitting the mission in hand too soon or prematurely thereby losing midway its perspective and objective.

j) Taking success for granted on the basis of gut feeling.

k) Feeling and expressing excessive confidence and being too much proud without doing proper planning, home work and appreciating actual scope and gravity of the mission/ task and your resource position and limitations.

Self-questioning

As you do introspection and self-assessment, you perform a self-addressed exercise with the noble purpose of Knowing Thyself. It reveals a canvas of your attributes and characteristics with strong and weak points and shows the scope for self-improvement and development thereby enabling you to adopt suitable corrective measures for overcoming your weak / negative areas as much as possible.

Since you thoroughly know yourself, it gives you a vivid, clear and specific picture for the adopting future course of action. The fact that you are now a conscious, knowledgeable and balanced person with a sense to think of pros and cons, your approach and course of action should be logical, systematic, deliberate, planned and thoughtful with your focused attention on achievement of your mission objective. Thus, it offers a favourable and encouraging picture with strong possibility for achieving success and avoiding losses or failure at any unexpected turn of events.

To make your task easier and to recapitulate the essence of this chapter, five basic salient questions are framed for you so that you can now ask yourself the end, the following questions.

a) Have you done your self-assessment and self-appraisal? Have you properly listed your strong and weak points? Do you want to adopt suitable measures for strengthening your strong points and correcting weak points?
b) Do you have strong driving and motivating force to work hard with urge for giving output to the best of your abilities?
c) Have you got willpower, confidence and vision for your future? Have you set any short and long term mission objectives?
d) Do you have strong urge for initiating the process of self-improvement and development? Do you like to consult and seek advice?
e) Are you aware about the availability of resources, support and patronage as required for achieving your mission in life? Are you willing, humble and ready to compromise your self pride, honour and ego if the support is required to be procured from outside sources?

Evaluation of Success

Success or successful act is that when you get / achieve what you wanted as a result of your planning, efforts and resources. As per life expectations, success is finally associated with achievement of desired wealth, power and fame or their combination. Every individual has his concept of success which could be a short term or long term goal. Short-term success is limited to immediate objective such as passing the final examination with merit or getting admission to a particular course or college. It varies from person to person according to his needs, family background, available means and resources.

The concept of success remains vague unless it is well defined and quantified as it is precisely done in industry for assessment of its annual performance.

There is always a base called bottom line and it is used as a reference line for comparing anything achieved thereafter with respect to this line. This reference line should be quite distinct and used as starting point for comparison in life.

There is no specific measure for quantifying success. So, it remains a subjective and abstract entity and it is left to your perception for judgement, assessment and satisfaction. Since it is compared with respect to the reference point, the present status is anyway expected to be high up and could be indicated in terms as 'high' or 'medium' or 'low'. It is thus possible to get an idea about the degree of success and if it is found fairly high, it should positively give pleasure and satisfaction on seeing your achievement of wealth or power or fame or their combination. It should however be noted that position of the reference line is very important factor. If its position is kept high up, then this comparison is likely to lead to unhappiness and frustration, despite your achievement of substantial and significant success under the given circumstances and resources. As a guideline, it should be left to your parents to consider your progress as you are making beginning to your career with their exclusive support.

Other side of success or achievement is philosophical and spiritual. Some people do not measure their success in getting honour, money, material possession, prestige and position as they give relatively very little importance to these materialistic values. Their concept of satisfaction is different. So, they look for getting love, friendship and mental satisfaction from their successful deeds. It is strange but it is true in case of certain persons who are dedicated and committed to the mission of development, upliftment and prosperity of the humanity and society. They never look to their comforts, interest and benefits and they derive their pleasure from service to the humanity of underprivileged people. Such persons although they belong to well off categories but remain free from evils such as lust, greed, dishonesty and envy. They give importance to the peace of mind by discovering their soul and spiritual fulfilment. They advocate that you should not become slave of the career and money but use them to improve the quality and dignity of your life.

There are certain parameters for perceiving happiness which are associated with your success. In fact, you should see whether achievement of success has given rise to these parameters in your life. These are given as under:

c) **Love**—For family members, friends, community, subordinates etc.
d) **Courage**—Moral courage and confidence to do what is right and just in your life and face problems and difficulties boldly and ingeniously.
e) **Freedom**—For doing your own things within the constraints for seeking autonomy, work flexibility, freedom of thought, expression and creativity from your career.
f) **Hope**—For being optimistic and overcoming your fears and anxieties.
g) **Lifelong Learning and Knowledge**—Remember that successful people never stop learning, listening and striving to be creative. Thus, your self development is a continuous process for achievement of progressive success.
h) **Self-esteem**—By following certain values and ethics that enable you to behave boldly and talk to your neighbouring people and friends with grace and dignity.
i) **Fun**—Progressive achievement of success should make your life exciting, joyous and pleasant.

Success is finally seen and experienced as a positive attitude of mind. You will be able see success even in failure because the positive attitude of your mind will look at failure as the seed of success to make a new beginning in future.

Evaluation of Failure

Occurrence of failure is interpreted as non achievement of the desired / intended / aimed objective of a mission / task / assignment /project after making adequate, deliberate and planned efforts and studies for its achievement. With this definition, what is significantly associated with failure is the mental and emotional state of mind of an individual who has to poignantly and silently bear it at the end. Besides, it generates an inferiority complex when it is judged with respect to those who succeed in execution of similar missions like success in competitive examinations.

Evaluation of any failure such as failing in higher secondary or graduate or competitive level examinations has to be examined and assessed vis-a-vis the studies and efforts whether they were carried out honestly, sincerely, truthfully and above all qualitatively and purposefully with the sense of dedication, involvement and commitment. The best person to evaluate his failure is the individual who can ascertain self centric and external causes after critically analysing the total episode by properly adopting the process of introspection. In this process, you should ask yourself some searching questions before concluding that the failure may be due to a cause beyond your control. These self-introspective questions which are addressed to you are indirectly related to your personal attributes and are mentioned below for finding the real causes:

a) Did you make honest and sincere studies and put in dedicated efforts?

b) Did you have a planned and systematic approach before commencement of the work?

c) Were you really dedicated and fully involved in your mission?

d) Were you committed to your mission and did you remain committed throughout?

e) Did you seek proper guidance and advice whenever faced with problems and difficulties? Did you act on it?

f) Were you free and frank in communication with your parents? Did you appraise your parents from time to time about your problems, difficulties and shortcomings whenever you came these across?

g) Did you face any serious financial problem in supporting your education and training?

h) Did you have an amenable and congenial environment for carrying out your studies?

i) Were you disturbed mentally or emotionally from your domestic or family side during your study period?

j) Did you face any health problems, causing pain or agony while studying?

k) Did you get disturbed by bad dreams?

l) Were you able to fully concentrate your attention on studies?

m) Did you carry any fear, tension or apprehension or worry or pressure on your mind?

This is how one should carry out introspection and try to evaluate failure in totality. External forces and causes should be considered and your failure should be attributed to them only after introspection is carried out and its evaluation is completed.

It should be remembered that the occurrence of the first or subsequent failure is never final in the life and is not the end. It is in fact the beginning, paving the way to success in your subsequent missions. What is required is to take the **failure gracefully and coolly and maintain a composed state of mind without getting disturbed emotionally and losing morale and courage.** Failure is caused due to your certain negative attributes, having played a dominant role without you being aware about them. As introspection distinctly brings them out, you can always adopt suitable remedial measures and neutralise their adverse effects.

It is now the elder's moral responsibility to pacify, console and bring back optimism to such candidates by offering them positive inspiring counselling and guidance. It is no doubt a difficult task but it has to be performed carefully and rationally in order to boost their morale and create hope for the bright future. In this respect, on such occasion, you may like to write to him a consoling letter and advocate him to carry out introspection according to the questionnaire as given above. Typical sum and substance of such a consoling letter is given in the Annexure 3 to this chapter for perusal.

(See Annexure 3 for the format of a typical consoling letter advocating intropection after occurrence of first failure in life).

5

The Role of Introspection in Facing Personal Interviews for Selection

SCOPE

1. What are the types of interviews?
2. What are the essential requirements for selecting a proper career?
3. What is the purpose of an interview?
4. What are the constraints of a public interview ?
5. What are an employer's demands and expectations from his employee?
6. What suitable actions should you take during the preparatory stage?
7. How do you go through the personal part of the interview?
8. What are the factors and aspects of your personality that are mainly observed and questioned?
9. What is the key factor in a public interview?

SERVICE ENVIRONMENT

After attaining suitable educational qualifications and professional training, every one of you looks for an employment in an organisation, institute or industry for adequate earning and having decent living. In fact, the aim of most young people is to seek a proper job or service after completing basic education and commence a service career. Some of them want to start their own business or small enterprise and become independent, self-reliant and enterprising. Due to proliferation of the educational institutes and while the number of the educated youth is increasing, availability of the jobs is shrinking and thus employment is progressively becoming difficult and highly competitive. In addition, due to the outstanding and tremendous technological developments in the fields of communication, information and computerisation which have affected all branches of commerce, engineering, transport, medical and others, the traditional job market has significantly started shrinking and those available are demanding high levels of skills, abilities and performance. Besides, there is neck to neck competition for earning excellent results with good quality products and thereby maintaining lead in low cost, high quality and corporate reputation. This has resulted in changing attitude, priorities and outlook of the employers towards their employees and the new standards of recruitment. You have got to take note of such a fast changing service scenario and its ever growing stringent demands in the field of employment and rising high quality job potential. You, as a candidate who wish to seek a job, can't afford to remain oblivious of the demands and challenges of the twenty-first century.

SCOPE

The subject of interview is quite vast and complex due to its many factors, each of a diverse nature. Entire exercise of interview appears unpredictable as there are no standard and universal practices, procedures and rules. Hence, this chapter is intended to offer you practical guidelines and some common sense measures so as to enable you to prepare for boldly facing different types of interviews. It is also aimed at developing confidence and reliance in yourself by adopting the process of introspection and self- assessment which demonstrates how it becomes useful and helpful to you by discovering strong and weak aspects of your personality as a whole.

While all multidimensional aspects of an interview can not be covered in this chapter, it is possible to describe the modality and process, pertaining to what actually happens in an interview and what could be the basis of questions which are likely to be framed by the members of the board. To this extent, this chapter will definitely offer you positive and real guidance and advice with emphasis on making realistic and meaningful preparation and building your self-confidence.

Types of Interviews

Interviews are conducted for assessing suitability of a candidate for induction into an organisation whose job and manpower structure is divided in different layers of operations, control and management such as:

a) **Basic working level.** For actual operation, on jobs, works. It is mostly the starting level of workers and engineers for induction after seeking a job.

b) **Middle supervisory and managerial level.** It is required for carrying out supervisory and managerial tasks at manager, senior manager and equivalent levels.

c) **High management level:** It is required for command and control functions of a Department / Division as its Head and mostly tenable by a deputy General Manager or its equivalent.

d) **Top level** as General Manager, Managing Director, Chairman or its equivalent.

Accordingly, ranks, grades and appointments are created in every organisation from the operational control and management point of view. Interviews are generally held for all appointments because of large number of applicants. Interviews are organised according to the qualitative requirements (QR) which vary from job to job according to the levels as stated above. Here, it is pointed out that induction at working level jobs is done through open advertisements but middle level appointments are generally filled by holding in-house departmental promotion committees which conduct in-house interviews and recommend suitable candidates for promotion. This normal departmental procedure adopted for making promotions and interviews has now become regular feature and integral part of the promotional process.

As stated in Chapter 3, your entire attributes of both positive and negative types are classified in three categories as essential, desirable and optional for various types of jobs and careers. Employer's eligibility criteria for the jobs are drafted accordingly. Now, irrespective of rank and post essential attributes which are classified as star qualities are required for all types of jobs and careers at working levels. Requirement for desirable qualities is felt as you intend to gain progressive promotions in your organisation's hierarchical structure at middle and senior level appointments. The need for optional qualities arises for appointments to high and top levels as head of department / division / organisation. You are therefore advised to prepare for interviews according to the level of induction and observe the guidelines and advice, given in subsequent paragraphs.

Essential Requirements for Selecting Any Service Career

Under the scenario of job environment as described above, you should not remain selective and complacent at the initial stage. You should not carry any inhibition or bias about a particular job and wait till the vacancy arises. In fact, whenever the opportunity comes to your way, you should never hesitate to grab it. Even though you fail to succeed, it offers you tremendous and valuable experience and exposure of going through the selection process. Of course, you should not act as a dare-devil but should know essential requirements of any service career so that it can help you to do proper preparation. In this respect, you are advised to take the following steps:

a) **Know the career/job market.** Keep an eye on what jobs are available and which organisations are the best to work with offering career prospects.

b) **Achievement of proper qualifications and professional training.** Achieve proper and higher educational qualifications and avail training facilities for different types of jobs. Try to gain some practical experience on job works and exposure to industrial practices and culture.

c) **Write a good self explanatory application form.** This is a very important document written by you about your Self, indicating your intention and what best abilities you can offer. You should highlight and emphasize those aspects of yourself which the employers are generally looking for such as experience, communication skill, quality consciousness, creative skill, commercial and economic awareness, integrity, time management and physical fitness and endurance.

d) **Prepare to project yourself effectively.** This pertains to your ability to express and communicate to your employer about your positive aspects and convey the impression that you would be an asset to his organisation. This depends upon how effectively and emphatically you project the positive aspects of your personality and performance.

e) **Maintain your professional image and functional rerputation.** This is important for getting the right jobs and you can't get easily pressurised to do illegal and unethical works.

f) **Keep learning and improving your knowledge.** This helps you to widen the scope of different jobs, assignments and mission works. Besides, it helps to extend your employability.

g) **Remain aware about the employer's needs and requirements.** It helps you to prepare for the interview and expect the questions accordingly. For this purpose, you should carefully examine the advertisement and its job requirements and also about the company's reputation and standing in the market.

h) **Never give up.** Continue your efforts and remain optimistic and positive in your approach to different types of jobs. Maintain calm and patience even if you miss one or two chances. Try again with vigour and force.

It should be noted that you should maintain a positive and constructive attitude and approach to any job or career. Your primary objective should be to gain experience and exposure while going through the selection process. In the bargain, you come across different types of employers, their job requirements and methods of selection. You eventually stand to gain tremendous experience and confidence to face any interview.

Purpose of Interview

Today, no job or career or entrance to a specialised professional course is possible without going through a selection process either written or oral face-to-face interview or both, especially for selection to the state or central government jobs. It offers an opportunity to a selection body to select the best ones from the lots available. This is possible only when the candidates who are already screened and found meeting the service criteria are personally and physically seen by the members of the selection board and subjected to questioning and intelligently observing their responses, reactions and overall personality. In this face-to-face meet with a candidate, his physical personality, body features, habits, body movements, conduct and mannerism are closely observed. He is asked such questions which are directed to ascertain his attitude, mindset, aptitude, relations, expression and thought process. The entire range of questions is generally and broadly found to cover various domains of his personality such as:

a) Mental make-up.
b) Emotional response.
c) Psyche related to his mindset, behaviour and relations.
d) Intellectual development (IQ, skills, uptakes, response).
e) Health condition (stamina, endurance, capacity for hard working).

These aspects will be further examined later.

Constraints of Interview

All of us have to appear for interviews for selection of a particular course or service immediately after passing or completing our academic course education or training. Today, even admission to an advanced course is not possible without giving an interview. The purpose of an interview is to select right and proper candidates according to the specified criteria of job specifications. In other words, it is a process of rejecting unsuitable and incompetent candidates from the screened lot as well as selection of the best possible among the lot of available candidates, actually appearing for the interview.

It is a direct meeting for a short duration between two divergent parties, one representing the selector, having wide scope and choice of selection and other side being you as a candidate with expectation for a job. The dice is heavily loaded against the candidates because of the following constraints of such modality in an interview:

1) **Availability of limited information.** Candidates do not have much information about the organisation except what is stated or published in the notice. They also do not know nature, trends, style, likes and dislikes of the members taking the interview.
2) **Shortage of time.** Each candidate is given a limited time for the interview and assessment has to be completed during this short allotted time. Members of the interview board are also busy people who are drawn from different departments having busy work schedules.
3) **Large number of candidates.** It is seen today that the number of applications and number of candidates appearing for interview against an advertisement is considerably large. The screening process and issuing call notices to eligible candidates have become difficult task.
4) **Different styles of biodata.** The prescribed format, if any for presenting bio data of the candidates does not always reveal the correct picture of the abilities of the candidates. It is difficult to assess since it is bound to contain excessive or boastful claims. Also, there is no standard technique for conducting oral / verbal interview and it depends mostly on moods, style, trends and occupancy state of the panel members.
5) **Verification.** There are no immediate means or scope to verify the statements and claims of the candidates except the original documents and perception of the interviewer. It is also difficult to assess genuineness of the original documents, especially related to experience and character certificates.
6) **Performance.** Your performance in the qualifying or written examinations and the way you have answered the

questions from members remain the only determining factors apart from your bio data.

7) **Type of members.** It depends a lot on the nature and abilities of members who are made available to take your interview. It is their experience, integrity, competence, maturity, knowledge and sharp observation power which will finally determine your selection despite your adequate qualifications and experience.

It is evident from the above that you as a candidate have to remain aware about these constraints and then organise and manage your preparation and presentation in an emphatic, convincing and realistic manner in order to score over your competitors. It is also necessary for you to know and anticipate what prominent attributes, the members are looking for and you have to find the best possible way of presenting them during that short period of the interview.

Awareness

You as a candidate who is genuinely interested in seeking a job have to appear before an interview board for selection. So, you have to maintain awareness on two fronts about the external forces as given below:

a) Criteria for Selection
b) Employer's Demands and Expectations

Criteria for Selection

Most of the employers state their selection criteria in their job advertisement. It basically pertains to required minimum educational qualifications and professional training about a particular job. You should always aim at qualifying yourself in this respect as there is no way of ignoring this essential requirement. There is also need about experience and exposure to a particular job environment so that you can easily adapt and adjust yourself. Employers do not wish to spend much on your training unless you are found suitable and adaptable to their requirements.

You must have the aptitude to do a particular job. Your response and urge to do and perform should be natural. You should examine your aptitude and find out what type of jobs suit you best and where you use your abilities in an optimum manner. If you do this exercise, you will be able to avoid mismatch and remain mentally prepared to face and project yourself accordingly. You must pay special attention to your family background and its financial position especially when you wish to appear for the competitive examinations at the state and national levels. Here, it takes a minimum of two to three years period in order to complete the process. Obviously, you should have adequate financial support. Besides, engineering and medical education has a very high fee structure. Unless you get a scholarship, you won't be able to manage if your parent's support is inadequate.

Finally, the most important factor is your health and physical fitness. If you wish to join Defence, Paramilitary services, your physical fitness matters a lot and you have to take a close look at your health condition. In fact, physical fitness is required for maintaining sound mind and concentration on the job. It ensures your stamina, endurance and capacity to work hard and continuously. Besides, it is manifested in your dignified actions such as walking, conduct, manners, performance, etc.

Employer's Demands and Expectations

While preparing for the interview, you should be conscious about the demands and expectations of your prospective employer who offers you employment and accepts your financial liabilities. He will invest in your training and prepare you for the job. Naturally, he is looking for certain qualities in your personality and ascertains whether you will be able to deliver the goods in a reliable and dependable manner. If you are aware about this requirement of any employer that he is definitely trying to look and assess for these attributes, you can have an edge over your competitors in the selection process. Now, what are those aspects that you should remember during your preparatory stage? These are given below.

a) Clear objective and vision about your future as a driving and steering force to your career.

b) Positive and healthy personality with minimum body movements, amiable behaviour, dignified conduct, cheerfulness, positive outlook and mindset, physical stamina for hard work.

c) Proper professional skill with adequate training and experience.

d) Application skill with an analytical approach for producing quality products.

e) Learning desire for improving your working skills and adopting new technical developments for ongoing works.

f) Focus on the job with no side attraction.

g) Loyalty and integrity to the employer and his organisation should be hundred percent.

h) Dedication and commitment to the works and your immediate boss.

i) Self-discipline in following rules, regulations and instructions without murmur.

j) Cost and quality consciousness for ensuring economical use of manpower and resources for giving quality output.

k) Work ethics and values for remaining away from vices, petty politics and agitations which hamper your performance and lower your output potential.

Preparatory Stage

With this background information, you should prepare yourself on all fronts after considering all types of eventualities. You should never take your interview lightly. You should face the interview with proper and systematic preparation with an eye on what an employer or his representatives in the selection board are expecting from you and looking for special qualities in you. You should anticipate questions of their interest in an interactive mode and encourage them for probing in your strong areas so that they come to know your potential, abilities and competence. So, proper planning and preparation with awareness about external forces are two prerequisites for success in an interview, group tests and selection boards. You should therefore take the following actions:

a) Study and understand given quantitative requirements (QR) for selection.

b) Study the job contents and required qualifications and experience.

c) Gather information about the company / organisation / Industry which has given the job advertisement such as its market position, product line, reputation, expectations, paying capacity, company objectives, etc.

d) Compare where your knowledge, skills, educational qualifications, experience and exposure qualify you for the job and make realistic assessment about your suitability.

e) Prepare carefully your curriculum vitae (CV) which is an account of your educational qualifications and previous occupations if any. Other areas of your positive qualities, strong points, knowledge and experience should be covered in self-introduction and resume. Project your positive assets in an objective manner.

f) Anticipate and identify the likely pattern of questions in an interview.

g) Build up your knowledge, seek guidance from competent persons and enquire from persons who have already faced similar interviews.

h) Assess the weak points / aspects of your personality and take proper remedial actions especially on your appearance, temperament, mindset, body movements, habits, dress and manners.

i) Assess the strong points / aspects of your personality. Think of how to project them.

j) Always think of the demands and expectations of an employer and keep them at the back of your mind.

k) Scan your educational and professional training periods and ascertain those areas where you have excelled in performance and they can constitute the strong points of your nature and character.

l) Practise a session of typical question-answer in order to improve your expression and the quality of your responses like voice which should be quite clear and audible.

m) Prepare yourself for the day of interview by having a proper dress, haircut, shave, shoes, etc.

It should be noted that the above preparatory measures are addressed to you. You should not carry any bias or reservation or question as to why they are required and why should I do. You should never allow your personal problems and shortcomings to come in the way of your preparation and incur handicap at the very starting level. You should maintain a calm, composed and cool temperament and never get excited, confused or jittery. Always remember that your proper and deliberate preparation will instill confidence in you and make you bold and courageous for facing the challenge of any interview.

PREPARATION OF CURRICULUM VITAE (CV)

This document is also commonly called a Self-Introduction or a Resume or a personal Bio-data form. It is a very important document as it offers first hand information about your education, professional skills, training, experience and personal characteristics. Your resume becomes a document of your own advertisement in the growing job-market. It is a soul of your job application and subsequent selection process. The resume should therefore be precise, concise, databased and factual. It should be drafted in such a way that it projects your truly glorified picture with emphasis on your key positive aspects such as professional skills and experience, relations, response level, honesty and integrity, work ethics and conduct. Being your personal advertising document, it should be carefully and judiciously drafted with specially chosen self-defining words.

It should be noted that screening of the candidates is primarily done on the basis of these documents received along with a large number of applications. Candidates who are found suitable in the screening process after carefully examining their resumes are called for interview. This document also serves as a guide for asking questions in order to verify and reveal the true picture of your potential, capabilities, talent and character. Thus, this document becomes a very important step in your qualifying and selection process. So, you should be tactful and judicious in emphasising the strong points of your nature, character, personality and performance without giving an impression of being boastful and exaggerated.

CONDUCT OF INTERVIEW

There are two parts of any interview. One pertains to the projection of your-self before the selection board members at the site of the interview. Another point pertains to what the members of the interview board expect from you on behalf of employers' specific expectations. Let us see the first part as to how you should project. Remember that this part creates an impression about your outward personality, upbringing, culture, values, ethics and morality and most of the members are likely to be either attracted or distracted by your first impression and influence. So, here are the tips for preparing yourself:

a) Be properly dressed and styled for the occasion.
b) Seek permission before entering the room. Walk gracefully toward your chair without making any unnecessary noise.
c) Pay compliments to all members in a humble manner by saying 'Good Morning or 'Good Afternoon, Sir'.
d) Look at the chairperson first and then at the other members of the interview panel while expressing the greetings.
e) Occupy the seat only when told or seek permission before sitting.
f) Sit straight and look confidently at the members in front.
g) Listen to questions carefully and answer them meticulously in audible and clear tone. Avoid fumbling for words. Add proper salutations like ' Sir ' or 'Madam' to your answers in response to questions.
h) Express yourself confidently. Say frankly NO if you don't know the answer instead of waffling.
i) Don't make any unnecessary body movements. Check your such habits that can cause an adverse impression.
j) Be humble, courteous and pleasant in your answers. Do not lose your temper or get irritated even if the question happens to be trivial, stupid and ridiculous or humiliating as it may be meant to assess your mental make-up, mindset and sensitivity to awkward situations.
k) Say Thank You and depart gracefully when the interview is over.

The second part is directed to actually assess your personal and performance oriented attributes.

Second Part through Oral Questions

The objective of this part is to find out your nature, character, mindset, behaviour, talent, potential, abilities, capacity and performance. While the members look at you as a candidate, physically present before them and observe your *Personality*, there is no other visible feature or means available to them for observation and assessment except your CV or resume or bio-data. Obviously, their questions will be directed at you to know your real worth and suitability for the job and cover generally the following areas:

a) Personality

b) Aptitude

c) Motivation

d) Vision

e) IQ

These are five driving factors in which the members are interested to know and find out their levels of possession by a candidate. The last factor IQ is already assessed from your academic performance and written test. So, most of the questions would be focused on various aspects of the above four main factors. You should therefore know what they are looking for in respect of these factors.

PERSONALITY

Your personality is the most prominent visible factor and is seen at a glance when you appear for the interview. It makes the first impression about yourself. This formation of the first opinion is an important process and can become a significantly decisive factor for final selection when there is close neck-to-neck competition among equally qualified candidates. Besides, an impressive personality can motivate the members to think or tilt their opinion in his / her favour.

Your personality has two dimensions, one pertains to its external features which are physically seen from outside and second pertains to its inner aspects which are normally manifested in the form of personal attributes, related to your inner personality. They are in fact responsible for describing your nature, character, relations, talent, conduct, temperament, potential and performance. Hence, your personality broadly covers two main dimensions, one that is seen by the people and another that needs to be assessed like prospects of your performance and career management.

When you participate in group discussion or group activities or appear for interview, your personality as a whole dimension is revealed, examined and tested on this platform. A group of attributes marked as Star qualities becomes evident at the first instant from your personality for judgement and assessment. It creates a distinct impression about your specific characteristics. It is further supplemented through discussion in the form of questions and answers. So, let us examine the first domain of your personality which is revealed in many forms as under:

Appearance

It includes your bearing, sharpness of features like size of forehead, eyes, nose, hair style, height, weight, body structure and general health. Face readers claim to know about your certain characteristics from your facial features. Large broad forehead, and large size of the skull associated with long nose and big eyes are generally presumed to be indicators of intelligence, sharp memory with quick grasping power and leadership traits. Small scintillating eyes with rapid eyeball movements are believed to indicate sharpness of judgement, skill, cleverness and perhaps a cunning approach. Over weight people are found slow at work. Lean and thin people are active, agile and suitable for outdoor works

Dress / Clothes

Dress should match your position, family background, education and more so to occasion. The approach should be to dress the way you want to be seen as an upright job seeker and not according to your own free taste or preference or fashion.

Behaviour and Manners

Your behaviour and manners reflect your background and upbringing. When you use simple words such as 'Sorry' and 'Thank you', they become indicators of your polite, gentle, humble, courteous and respectful nature and sensitive feelings for others. Besides, your style of response and manner of expressing your views especially when you do not agree or wish to negate indicate your maturity. Your body movements like shaking of a hand or head or looking somewhere reveal a specific language and become indicators of your restlessness, fickleness, confusion and lack of concentration.

Speech and Voice

What you say and the way you say trigger opinion formation for or against you. Grammatical mistakes in your expression will reflect on poor quality of your education. Your accent and flow of words should be natural and steady. Any twisted or thick accent in your expression creates negative impression about you. The way you speak and express should show your thinking process. The tonal quality of your voice also makes a significant difference.

Teeth

People are found to judge you by what they see in your mouth. Big canine teeth can make you look aggressive and buck teeth can make you look stupid. Hence, attention should be given to correct them so as to project your pleasing and impressive image. Of course, cosmetic treatment in this regard is not essential, but why should you not go for it if it is within your means?

Performance

This is generally examined and observed when you participate in group activities like discussion, joint or individual assignment and project work. Similarly, you are given an outdoor task or exercise and a go-ahead signal. The factors which form part of your inner personality are carefully and minutely watched and noted are as under:

— Initiative, awareness, systematic planning, support, cooperation, team spirit, envious and grabbing nature, perseverance, optimism, forward outlook, courage and boldness for facing challenges, leadership, casualness, indifference, seriousness. dedication, responsibility and commitment, rigidity, firmness, concentration and focus, stability, involvement, sense of timing, loyalty and integrity.

Intelligence

This is judged and assessed from the way you give answers and solutions to queries and to the questions from members, apart from your performance in written tests and results from school / college annual examinations. Remember that intelligent practical approach is appreciated more than a bookish or textbook approach.

Self-Control and Temperament

This is evident and judged from your responses to provocative, confusing, tricky and random questions and from your behavior under difficult situation in group / project activities. It indicates your emotive feelings, sensitivity, irritation, cool and calmness, endurance, and level of tolerance while working under difficult and adverse conditions.

Body Language

Understanding of body language is the recent technique which has entered the human resource management field and is being used for judging and assessing the people when you see and watch them in your face to face meeting during discussion or interview. You can simply watch the body movements of the person and sense certain behavioural parameters by your close observation and judgement. You can assess and draw your conclusions from such physical movements of the persons who are totally ignorant and unaware about the signals transmitted by their movements and decoded by the other party whom they are encountering in a meeting or dialogue or interview.

This technique is now being adopted by the interview boards for assessing certain attributes of your personality. It is now combined with the personality test and seen in totality. As the candidate enters and interview starts, members of the board observe his personality and body movements and start decoding the body language. The candidates are totally unaware about their own movements which may be natural or deliberate and caused by the interaction during the interview.

It is proposed to make the candidates aware about this new aspect of their personality. They should keep in mind and remain conscious about it in natural way. This issue cannot be ignored or avoided. While preparing and improving your personality, you should take this aspect into consideration. These body movements may appear simple and unintentional but mean a lot to those who understand body language. They are identified and mentioned below along with their meaning which is conveyed to the other party.

1. **Folded arms**—Reflects defensiveness.
2. **Firm handshake**—Reflects a decisive person.
3. **Steady eye contact**—Reflects openness and trust.
4. **Passive face avoiding direct eye contact**—Shows unbalanced and uncomfortable state of mind.
5. **Gestures like clenched fist, pointing index finger or hand**—Shows aggressiveness.
6. **Smile on the face and relaxed state**—Readiness to communicate openly and sincerely.
7. **Crossing of arms or legs or avoiding direct eye contact, or sitting on the edge of the chair or touching face, nose, ears, chin often**— Indicates falsehood, wrong and incorrectness in statements.
8. **Rubbing hands vigorously**—Indicates pleasurable sense of expectations or satisfaction.
9. **Scratching the head**—Indicates confusion, doubt, uncertainty.
10. **Both hands behind the head**—Indicates superiority, confidence and possible arrogance.
11. **Rubbing of chin**—Indicates that your ideas are being given careful consideration or thinking process is on.
12. **Head resting on hand**—Indicates boredom or fatigue.
13. **Clenched hands when speaking**—What is being talked or discussed about is frustrating.
14. **Clenched hands when listening**—The listener is responding negatively.
15. **Arms folded with thumbs pointing upwards**—Indicates nearly impossible to convince.
16. **Hands pressed together as in prayer**—A desire to persuade or underline a point gently but firmly.

It is pointed out that a few of the visible factors as stated above may make difference to your selection as it depends upon the members to understand their meaning and implications. Body language and its role in interpreting your personality have recently assumed significance and therefore this aspect cannot be ignored in your preparation for an interview.

Personality Development

Hence, apart from brushing knowledge and professional skills while preparing for the interview, you must pay also special attention to the visible factors of your personality and adopt such steps and measures so as to improve and enhance your personality. It should be remembered that visible factors of your personality reveal a lot of your personal information of positive and negative types that enables the members to assess your suitability or otherwise during a short period of face to face interview.

It is therefore advisable to be aware and remain conscious of various aspects of your personality. In fact, a large number of courses and programs are available in the market for development of your personality factor. Many pertinent and concerned aspects have already been covered and stated under the heading of Self-Development Process in Chapter 4 of this book.

Aptitude

It addresses to your innate talent, capacity, urge and willingness to learn, work and perform. It implies your mental adaptability and power to select a particular course or career and seriously pursue with total involvement and commitment for achieving success. In other words, aptitude refers to your innate ability to be able to do the best in areas of your interest and liking. This innate ability is not affected by external forces such as learning and training. As such, your mental response is genuine, natural and spontaneous.

Since it deals basically with your natural urge and liking, it determines your voluntary and spontaneous response to a particular career /course. Being natural adoption by mind, it enhances your uptake and assimilation for giving maximum output from your personal attributes.

As regards judging your aptitude in a practical way, different types of presentations are given before you. Your response in terms of corresponding answers as given by you to each presentation is noted and tabulated. The presentation covers the following types of dimensions:

- Visual, numerical, verbal, sequential, spatial, vocal and three-dimensional

Suppose your response to numerical type of presentation is found the highest. Then your aptitude will be for careers like Accountancy, banking, audit, costing. If it happens to three-dimensional view, then aptitude will be for careers like fine or commercial art, painting, advertising and so. Thus, your aptitude may be found the highest to one of many presentations which is related to a particular career / course and relatively less to others. The choice and final selection is then left to you. Efforts are made in an interview to find out your aptitude for a job offered to you. There is no point in selecting you for a job for which you have no aptitude.

Aptitude and I Q (Intelligence Quotient) are correlated as each pertains to certain innate qualities which remain unaffected by external forces as stated above. It definitely provides a measure of giving maximum output if a person is given a career of his choice wherein his aptitude lies.

Motivation

It is a natural force, emanating from within yourself or instilled in you that appeal to your senses to act on their own. It is an act of your mind to focus your potential and energies for undertaking and following a particular career or course in which you are likely to do your best and finally achieve success at the end. Motivation constitutes a force to drive you to act and pursue a particular direction. It is an inborn urge and a strong feeling or an idea hammered into you that prompts you to act purposefully and pursue a particular activity to its logical end. It implies planning a systematic approach and timely action along with hard work and perseverance.

Motivation addresses to your mental faculties for concentrating your efforts and directing your energies for achieving a particular objective. It enables your mind to focus on a specific job effectively. Thus, motivation is essential in order to achieve the end result under the most difficult situation, laced with problems. You are often given a detailed briefing and are appraised about the purpose and utility of a mission or project. Preaching, training, sermon and briefing are the general means adopted for motivating you. Thus, this can be the product of some one's expertise in command, expression and delivery

Vision

Your vision means the capability to think and formulate the plans and goals for achievement in future. It aims at your abilities to have forethought and foresight about your future career oriented events. In a simple way, it amounts to state your dream of what you would like to be in future when the right opportunity is given to you. It also means to set your mission for the future such that you can organise and execute your activities and performance for proceeding in specific direction. When it is enquired about your vision in an interview, the intention is to ascertain whether you have set any goal and are prepared to steer and drive yourself towards your destination.

To begin with, a vision at the level of working posts and jobs is not material and significant as the focus is to find out your suitability for performance of a specific job effectively and efficiently. But, as you grow and have a few years of service and look for promotions, your mature vision makes a difference to the interest of your employer and his organisation. Here, the need arises to have self-driven and motivated persons to perform and substantially contribute to an organisation. Thus, vision of an employee who is set on the path of promotions becomes a significant contributory factor and asset for the interest of an organisation.

Awkward Questioning

You are cautioned to expect some awkward, frivolous and sometime ridiculous questions from some members of the board. These questions do not apparently have any relation or relevance to your job but they are thrown at you in a casual manner in order to assess your response, reaction and temperament. You should maintain your posture cool and composed, think over and answer them in a positive manner. You should be serious and polite in taking them on and answer them in a logical and rational manner. You should never treat the question stupid nor show your negative reaction. In case, you don't know the answer say frankly, 'Sorry, I don't know'. In case, the question happens to be controversial, you should refrain from expressing your firm opinion but show in your answer that you are aware about the 'for and against' arguments relating to the controversy. If you are not fully aware then say, 'Sorry, I do not wish to comment. Here, you are advised not to waffle and boast. Some board members may divert your attention to current political scenario and test your general knowledge and find out your mental alertness for reaction to different scenarios. You should remember that these awkward questions are thrown at you like a spitfire with the purpose of ascertaining your psychic frame of mind and mental make up. You should naturally be prepared for such eventualities.

Introspection and Self-assessment

You should note that the process of introspection and self-assessment plays a very important role in discovering your personal attributes of both positive and negative types as stated under the above stated paragraph headings. The exercise is addressed to yourself and it helps you in a way to establish your identity and project it effectively and affirmatively. It is always pragmatic to look at yourself from employer's point of view as it brings purposefulness, objectivity and realism in your preparation for the interview and more so in establishing your edge in selection over others. Here, you approach the interview with full awareness and consciousness about the employment market scenario and employer's expectations. In the process, you have perceived yourself in the role and position of your employer. Obviously, you will face the interview with confidence and conviction that will be reflected in your answers.

Key Factor – Self-confidence

As you go through the process of preparation on the basis of your Introspection and self-assessment, you are definitely poised to gain trust in yourself. In this process, you get revelation of your inner power, strength, potential, abilities and skills. You also come to know certain shortcomings of your personality and weak areas of your nature and habits which you would now like to correct and control in order to overcome their ill effects on your selection prospects in the interview. Thus, this entire process if properly, sincerely and meticulously executed is bound to enable you to gain strong confidence in yourself. As a result, you can appear for the interview with full confidence and clear vision. Incidentally, your facial expression and body language will reveal your confidence and indicate that you have absolute control over your abilities. Since you have properly and deliberately prepared for the interview with due appreciation of the entire situation, your self-confidence is well justified.

Finally, it is pointed out that it is only your personal responsibility for getting selected in the interview. All relevant useful information and guidance are given in this chapter for enabling you to become successful. Since the scope of any interview is vast and unpredictable, wisdom and discretion dictate in preparing yourself on the basis of introspection and self-assessment. You get total perspective of the entire process. And even if you don't make it in a particular interview, you don't lose much and your preparation becomes handy for the next interview which you will perhaps face with redoubled energy, strength, experience and of course confidence.

The Essence of the Personal Interview

a) Selection and placement in any job is possible only through the interview against published or otherwise made known vacancies and job requirements.

b) The public interview process has certain drawbacks and candidates should be aware of them while preparing for it.

c) Personality, aptitude, motivation, vision and I.Q. are the main parameters which are generally considered for assessment of any candidate. Questions pertaining to these aspects are asked by the members of the board.

d) Your personality plays a dominant role since it is a visible factor that causes impression and influence on the members at the first glance. You should take cognisance of various personality related factors while preparing for the interview.

e) You should adopt the process of Introspection and self-assessment for gaining self-confidence. You should always approach interview with full confidence and proper preparation.

f) Even if you don't make it, do not get upset and discouraged. The experience, knowledge and wisdom gained in this interview will definitely be useful and helpful to you in your subsequent interviews.

6

The Role of Introspection in Managing Your Service Career for Promotions and Advancement

SCOPE

1. What is the need for managing your service career?
2. What are the expectations of your employer from you?
3. What is the Annual Confidential Report? What is the basis for writing this Report?
4. How will you assess and judge your Performance?
5. What are your performance oriented attributes?
6. What types of professional skills do you need to acquire in your career?
7. How will you deliver effective performance?
8. How will you maintain positive attitude?
9. What are the guidelines for career advancement?
10. What type of management techniques do you need to adopt for achieving high level career advancement?
11. What are the precautions and warning signals that you need to observe against pitfalls?
12. What are the challenges of the twenty-first century to your service career?

Practical Aspects

In the previous chapter, you have seen one of the practical aspects of Introspection where you find that it plays a significant role in appraising you about your own potential, capabilities, abilities and indirectly motivating you to adjust and prepare yourself in meeting expectations of the Selection Boards. These employment agencies have certain specific service oriented requirements and expectations from the candidates who should fit into their service network and organisational structure, be productive and finally deliver the profitable results. So, they are very specific and particular to ensure that the candidates recruited have certain basic positive attributes like diligence, endurance, aptitude, motivation, will power, dependability, dedication and vision. These positive attributes drive them to work hard, honestly and sincerely with a mission orientation, self-driven approach and dedication.

So, it becomes incumbent and compulsory on your part to ensure that you should try to meet those expectations. In fact, efforts are made through the means of written or oral tests or both to assess the presence of the attributes corresponding to their expectations from you. It is therefore obvious that you should make all possible efforts to demonstrate that you do possess them as much as they expect or as much as they need for the jobs / services. The fact that you are aware and conscious of an employer's needs and expectations makes a lot of difference in your approach, planning and preparation for the impending interview.

Scope

The subject under this chapter is applicable to those candidates who are already in service and have put in a few years of service in the organisation. They will obviously start expecting promotions in rank and advancement in status after putting specified years of service from the day of initial recruitment. The organisation may be government semi government/ public sector undertakings / industries where the candidates are selected properly and carefully through a tedious procedure after considering their qualifications and grading in academics along with performance in interviews. While selecting a candidate, his mental abilities, aptitude, attitude and star attributes are assessed in order to find suitability and usefulness for an organisation.

Purpose

Now, you go a step further. After your selection and getting employment in a particular organisation / industry, your service tenure which means your service career actually and really starts and you are now poised on the doorstep of your destiny which awaits with open hands to shower on you the fruits of your work, performance, conduct, relation and professional skills during your service career.

Here is a big question. Should you handle your job and career with a blind and casual approach and be happy with whatever you earn for your living and survival? With your educational and professional background and instinctive and inspirational feelings, it is natural that you certainly and genuinely want facilities, comforts and luxuries for living which should accrue from your career in which you are presently employed.

Now, the question comes up. How and in what way? Need for Service Career Management

You will definitely ask a few questions such as:

- **Why is there a need to manage my career?**
- **What is the purpose in managing my career?**
- **How does it help in achieving my cherished goals and objectives?**

Well, these are legitimate questions and doubts. You are therefore reminded that at this time, you are working in an organisation in a highly competitive environment where the emphasis is on the result oriented performance and maintaining financial lead and stability of your organisation, company / industry. You are working in a group, team, section and you are very much part of them in all respects. So, you are individually and collectively responsible for its performance as a whole. Apart from organisation's overall benefits and prosperity, your personal prosperity is also involved in the following ways as under :

a) Receiving regular pay packet for your comfortable living with no cuts.

b) Receiving annual pay rise and increments as per the cost of living.

c) Receiving progressive promotions to higher ranks with higher efficiency, responsibilities and status.

d) Receiving placements in different jobs and assignments of responsibilities of different sections and departments for getting multidisciplinary more comprehensive experience.

e) Receiving wide experience and exposure for seeking diversity in various careers of different types.

f) Becoming the key performer and highly dependent asset to the organisation.

Conduct of Service Career

Obviously, you have to perform and do well. You have to become an important part of an organisation. You are required to deal with persons from different departments. You have to behave in gentle and polite manner, follow instructions and comply with the rules and regulations of the management and supervisory staff. You have to report completion of your performance and maintain its quality. While you do so and perform, you have to be aware and conscious that your personal attributes are indirectly playing a significant positive or negative role and your demonstrative performance is being affected and influenced accordingly. You should note the fact that your positive attributes boost and enhance your performance and your negative attributes like anger, greed, ego, temperament, casualness, negative mindset, indifference, etc. retard and regress your performance. You should further know that your performance is being continuously watched and monitored by your superior officials and your annual performance report is written accordingly.

Initial Service Period

In this period of service, a candidate is on probation. It may be for one are or extended further, depending upon his conduct, response and performance. The candidate gets an opportunity to serve under supervisors in all departments on rotational basis. His performance, grasp, style of functioning and uptake abilities are observed closely and minutely and he is confirmed for retention in service only after getting satisfactory reports from the concerned superiors. This initial period of service is therefore very important and crucial for future of the candidate. Hence, candidates should remain alert, conscious, aware and dutiful and demonstrate their personal attributes during daily functioning. Once confirmed in service, it is expected that the tempo and momentum of their probationary service period should remain and be maintained in later part of the service. During this period, you should clearly and carefully understand the needs and expectations of your employer.

Awareness of Employer's Expectations

You are given an employment for doing a specific job in an organisation. Your employer has accepted the liability of regularly paying you the notified salary and allowances. Here, the most important issue to remember is that if your employer survives, you survive and that depends upon how efficiently and effectively you work and give your expected output. With such an interactive, interdependent and inter- personal relationship, your employer has to firstly survive and make profit so that he can offer you salary regularly with other benefits like a promotion. Now, an employer having his interest primarily in his mind, he has natural expectations from his employees. Interviews and selection process are today recognised platforms where employer tries to search and ascertain certain functionally qualifying parameters which he mentions in his job advertisement and looks to find in candidates at the time of interview. Now, you have to give due importance and credence to your employer's expectations from you. You should know those expectations and personally ascertain how far you will be able to meet them. These are given below for your serious and sincere consideration:

a) Goal / Objective set for your personal career advancement.
b) Drive and motivation to work for your employer's objective.
c) Professional skills for different types of jobs.

d) Keenness and willingness for improving and updating your professional skills.
e) Loyalty and integrity for the organisation.
f) Cost and quality consciousness.
g) Healthy work ethics and team spirit.
h) Focus on job, quality, output and company's interest.
i) Keenness to learn new jobs and shoulder additional responsibilities.
j) Effective expression, both verbal and written.
k) Patience, politeness and gentleness.
l) Time consciousness.
m) Leadership of a small group, team, mission, project.

It is obvious that your employer will try to ascertain above whether you have the qualities by asking you pointed and leading questions during interview and subsequently by observing you for demonstrating them in your performance.

Annual Confidential Report (ACR)

This is a powerful document which provides a unique means to your employer for closely assessing your performance. Accordingly as per the procedure, your head of the department has to annually report in writing in the specific format on your performance. This reporting covers your personal attributes of both positive and negative types, demonstrative performance and results achieved. For this purpose, you are being observed continuously and closely by your immediate superior officials (Reporting officials) and periodic reports are submitted confidentially to the Head in the standard format. The layout can be on the lines of specimen as given in the Annexure 4 to this chapter according to the laid down procedure by the Personnel and Manpower Department. (See Annexure 4 for the format of an ACR).

Promotional Stages

In every organisation, there is a specified structural hierarchy of management, consisting of various ranks and status which eventually leads to the top position. A candidate is promoted to the next rank after completing specific period of service or as and when vacancy arises if found suitable. For this purpose, the Promotion Board examines thoroughly your personal records, particularly Annual Confidential Reports on you.

The criteria for promotions are laid down by the organisation. Your personal Star and Star Plus qualities and your performance as demonstrated along with the useful results as reported in your ACRs are deeply considered and cross checked with respective heads for confirmation and recommendation. The candidate is cleared for promotion only thereafter. This procedure is adopted at every stage of promotion to higher ranks. The criteria for promotion to senior and higher ranks start getting more stringent and cover much wider and finer areas of nature, personality and performance as demanded by the responsibility and accountability associated with high ranks.

Performance

All these personal expectations and desires can be fulfilled only when you perform well and your performance is recognised for its importance, quality, relevance and positive contribution to your organisation. Your performance is a demonstrative visible activity and seen by all persons including your supervisory officials. While performing, you indirectly demonstrate your personal attributes of both positive and negative types. Thus, your performance gets affected positively or negatively and assessment about your performance in quality and substance is done accordingly. Here, it is strongly advocated that you should do your own assessment in order to ascertain your suitability for the job, responsibilities and place into the hierarchical structure of your organisation. For this purpose, it is opportune time to specifically ask certain performance oriented introspective questions to yourself such as:

a) Have I got proper qualifications and experience for the job I am selected for?

b) Do I keep myself updated with the latest development and technology in my field by attending seminars, workshops, tutorials as and when held and also through my personal efforts?

c) Am I really playing the key role so as to be called 'dependable' from the view point of my boss while discharging my responsibilities of diverse nature?
d) Do I try to shoulder additional responsibilities without having told specifically told, thereby showing my initiative and willingness?
e) Do I support my boss wholly and willingly without questioning his authority?
f) Do I plan for continuous learning in order to increase my knowledge and wisdom?
g) Do I seek advice from the competent persons without any hesitation whenever I get stuck?
h) Do I observe proper and effective time management system? Do I always complete my job or assignment within the given time schedule and need no reminders?
i) Do I voluntarily participate in the group discussion, panel discussion, brain storming sessions and periodic meetings?
j) Do I maintain social contacts, relations and develop interaction with persons of different classes, professions and levels?
k) Am I a patient, good interactive listener and try to get feedback on my performance?
l) Am I humble, cordial and amiable in my behaviour, conduct and relations?
m) Do I often get angry or irritated or lose my temper whenever any unpleasant thing happens?
n) Do I have ego or do I boast about my performance and do I talk much about my achievements?
o) Do I try to evade my responsibility and pass the buck to somebody else?

Incidentally, this is also the way of writing your own Personal Performance Report by you on your performance. In fact, you get an opportunity for critically examining your actual performance and ascertain if it is up to the mark as expected by standard norms. You will obviously find that your actual performance is related to some of your personal attributes out of the list as given in the next paragraph, and eventually depends upon how many of them you possess and in what proportion. Such type of personal assessment, if done honestly and sincerely, will certainly help you and clarify most of your doubts, complaints and grudges about your superior officers if you happen to miss the bus for promotion.

Observation about Your Performance-oriented Personal Attributes

These are some important performance related questions which cover the official, social, ethical and behavioral aspects of your life. Here, you are interrogating yourself and seeking honest, truthful answers for your own information and assessment. Once you get answers to these questions, some affirmative and some negative, your positive and certain negative attributes are also revealed and they really determine the benchmark for your self-assessment, performance and achievement. The list of self-addressed interrogative questions is given below:

a) Do I have willingness and positive attitude to perform?
b) Am I competent and suitable for jobs of higher grades?
c) Do I have enough drive and motivation?
d) Do I have foresight and vision for the future?.
e) Do I have a sense of self-responsibility and Self esteem?
f) Am I totally dedicatd and commitmed to work?
g) Do I always concentrate on my duties and responsibilities?
h) Am I time conscious for completion of my work schedule?
i) Am I calm, composed and have quiet nature?
j) Do I work with team spirit, cooperation and togetherness?
k) Have I got tolerance, endurance and mental toughness?
l) Do I behave with politeness, gentleness and amiability?
m) Am I thoughtful and patient in listening to others without any provocative reaction?
n) Am I inquisitive, searching and curious for gaining knowledge and wisdom?

o) Do I have a non-vindictive, non-reactive and non-provocative attitude even while facing criticism or adverse remarks?

p) Am I egoistic, boastful and arrogant and liking self-eulogy?

q) Am I bold and courageous in taking risks and facing challenges?

r) Do I have self-confidence and sel-reliance?

s) Am I temperamental and hyper-sensitive?

t) Do I have emotional, irritating, restless and casual attitude?

u) Am I selfish, greedy and indifferent?

v) Am I arrogant and adamant in my expression?

w) Do I possess a mindset for thinking positively or negatively?

x) Am I flexible in my viewpoints, thoughts and approach?

This is a long list of positive and negative attributes. They become evident and clear to you from your self-introspective interrogation exercise. It actually aims at probing your performance for ensuring quantity, quality, standard, style, relevance and finally objectivity in contribution and self-achievement. Once you get the answer as yes or no regarding presence in yourself against each attribute, you should ask the next question as to how much. The answers reveal the quantitative remarks such as strong, high, average, and poor or none for presence of each attribute thereby making your peformance related assessment a complete exercise.

Well, you are now in a the position to truly assess your performance in light of the treasure of your positive and negative attributes which have obvious bearing and influence on the quality and standard of your performance. Here, you become the first Judge and you come to know about your performance. At the same time, you come to know the strong and weak points of your Self and you can certainly think of their positive or negative impact on your performance. Before it gets adversely affected, you can prudently and judiciously take remedial and corrective actions so as to avoid ill effects of your negative attributes on your performance and consequent damage to your career. At the same time, you become aware of your strong attributes which offer you moral and natural strength and enhance your power and potential. Obviously, it results in boosting your performance and consequently improving your career prospects.

This is the direct substantial advantage you gain from the self addressed exercise of Introspection and self-assessment done mid-term or at the end of the period while the performance year is in progress.

Different Roles in Performance

Besides the importance and relevance of your basic performance, you are required to perform different roles with different functions, duties and responsibilities. They need different skills, training, knowledge, experience and exposure. You have to show your proficiency, competence and suitability in these roles. So, you have to really prepare and train yourself under someone's guidance. Besides, you should know the demands of each role and its characteristics. Let us take a look at those roles as under:

a) Supervisor / Superintendent.

b) Head of the Section / Department / Group.

c) Executive / Administrator / Controller.

d) Organiser / Policy maker / Co-ordinator .

e) Event Manager.

f) Teammate / Subordinate./ Team Leader.

g) Group / Mission / Project Leader.

h) Speaker / Lecturer / Teacher.

i) Advisor / Counsellor.

j) Student / Candidate while attending training courses, workshops, etc.

k) Negotiator.

It should be noted that while performing in different roles, you need to demonstrate your different personal attributes for making your role effective and result oriented. Your performance and its success depend upon your personal qualities like leadership, positive mindset, motivation, vision, professional knowledge, behavior and conduct. You have to maintain your cool and be composed, patient, responsive and interactive in your relations.

Development of Skills

There are two types of skills, one is called Hard Skills (Cognitive) and another is called Soft Skills (Non-Cognitive). Hard skills are also referred to as "On the Job Skills" pertain to your professional knowledge which you gain by going through various professional training courses in specific fields in a proper training institute. It enables you to perform your specific job for which you are specifically employed. It is basically at the working level. So, you have to learn a new job whenever you are shifted to another one or when you join another organisation which deals with different works or products or projects. Here, the skill of an individual worker is not transferable and he has to learn again for handling a new job.

Non-cognitive skills refer to your abilities and potential for organising, controlling, managing, administrating and conducting various functions and activities. These are basically personal attributes and functionally related to your personal skills. These are described in Management Parlance as under:

a) Behaviour, Conduct and Values
b) Personal Characteristics
c) Intellectual Abilities
d) Performance and Stability
e) Work Motivation
f) Interpersonal Skills
g) Administrative Skills

So, they are called Soft Skills. These are achieved over a period while serving in different roles in different organisations under different working conditions. Here, your personal, especially positive attributes play a special role in enabling you to respond, absorb, assimilate and communicate them properly and effectively. These skills are eventually transferable. So, when you join a new organisation, you carry these skills with you in the form of your experience and knowledge as your personal baggage and you find them useful there in similar ways as before. There is a requirement of marginal change in approach and style which depends upon different environmental, geographical and demographic conditions. Of course, these skills are required for appointments at senior and higher levels and your valuation in a new organisation is done on the basis of the depth of your professional knowledge, experience, exposure and achievements for handling different types of managerial jobs.

Hence, it is essential that you should be aware about these types of skills and their demands. You should therefore focus your attention and efforts in developing these skills confidently and competently at the earliest so that you shortly become an effective performer and achiever under different operational, organisational and administrative controls and conditions.

Prominent Attributes for Effective Performance

When you begin your service career, you come across different working stages at different times and levels of command and control functions. Besides, you come across different supervisory and officiating persons of different temperaments at working and management levels as immediate and superior bosses as well as subordinates and colleagues. As a result, there is a continuous demand on your personal qualities in order to demonstrate your talent and effective performance, working, behaviour and relations. On the other hand, your employer expects you to deliver a result oriented performance and become soon an effective team member and asset to his organisation. How should you match the situation so that both parties are finally benefited? For this purpose, there is a need for you to possess the following positive attributes:

a) Integrity, self-discipline and values.
b) Adaptability to get along with others.
c) Industriousness, i.e., hardwork, diligence and perseverance.
d) Honesty, sincerity and truthfulness.
e) Politeness, amiability and gentleness.
f) Determination, firmness, steadiness, consistency and mission orientation.

g) Dedication, devotion, involvement, responsibility and accountability.
h) Dependability and commitment.
i) Time-consciousness, promptness and initiative.
j) Drive and motivation.
k) Communication skill in expression for group activities, discussion and reporting.
l) Professional competence and creativity.
m) Credibility and respectfulness for management.
n) Ethics, etiquettes and work culture.

You should note that your immediate and superior bosses expect you to possess the above stated qualities and they try to assess your performance in view of these qualities. Whenever you perform as per their expectations, they are happy and try to grade you for higher progressive promotions and appointments. Accordingly, you receive good annual confidential reports and recommendations for higher promotions.

What is important to note in this exercise is that your performance is the key factor directly responsible for career progression and indirectly your personal attributes also which ultimately speak for the quality, relevance and contribution of your performance.

Special Tips for Managing Your Service Career

While you perform and interact with many persons of different professional skills and classes, you face incidents and demanding situations. Each may be different and require different skills and techniques for handling and managing. While it may not be possible to cover and cater to all sorts of occurrences, you should have certain tips for skilfully managing them and overcoming the difficult ones with the least amount of damage and loss. Thus, you remain aware and vigilant for reacting to such situations in a positive manner. What are those practical tips? They are enumerated below:

a) Follow the path of trust, efforts, attitude and motivation which are identifiable by a single word called Team.

b) Form a good team or group with high level of team spirit, cooperation and attachment.

c) Emphasize on your effective professional and communication skills. Avoid jumping to conclusion and preconceived ideas.

d) Use your body language to your best advantage.

e) Develop active listening technique for gathering information, ideas and suggestions. Be patient, serious and a good listener with occasional encouragement to the talker.

f) Avoid giving advice. Be specific to your needs while directing, commanding and monitoring.

g) Maintain self esteem and a balanced attitude with humility, sincerity and politeness.

h) Avoid ego and boastful talking. Also avoid saying that I am busy and I did it.

i) Adopt self-evaluation technique at different stages of your performance.

j) Observe effective time management and be punctual.

k) Adopt always positive mental attitude.

l) Be always a Mountain Mover and not a Mountain Creator.

m) Adopt continuous learning technique and remain well informed, well versed and updated.

n) Avoid in-house politics and criticism of organisation's rules and regulations.

o) Remain away from vices and anti-social, anti-company elements. Also stay away from union politics.

Steps to Maintain a Positive Attitude

There is a requirement for maintaining your positive mental attitude. This is associated with your positive mindset and taking things in positive strides. In fact, this is a way how you can become happy, joyous and cheerful and maintain calm, composed and cool posture. You also avoid your immediate emotive and volatile reaction and initiate positive thought process for tackling the unpleasant situation. You eventually avoid your nervous breakdown and save the situation by not-complicating it. So what are those steps that you should adopt ? These are listed below:

a) Develop a positive self-image.

b) Develop confidence and trust in your abilities and potential.

c) Avoid criticism, foul language and negative remarks and thus create a positive environment.

d) Arrange and plan your approach and activities properly, thoroughly and meticulously with anticipation for possible pitfall.

e) Banish the thoughts on past events. Refer them only to learn from mistakes and errors committed and take their positive cognisance.

f) Believe consciously in what you are doing with due consideration to its relevance and organisational interest.

g) Seek the advice of your superiors whenever in doubt.

h) Always maintain your high morale, ethics, values and conviction in your positive thought process and action.

i) Read books on various topics and subjects and improve your knowledge, outlook, vision and thought process.

j) Program your subconscious mood, attitude, behaviour and habits in positive manner.

Career Diversification

In simple words, it means change of job or service from one organisation to another at a different location or may be in the same location in mega cities or metros. Such a change offers different working environments with different people and divergent corporate objectives along with different systems and procedures involving resource, human and financial managements. It is advisable to change jobs especially at an early stage in order to get full exposure and experience over a wide spectrum of activities and job schedules. Sticking to one job creates monotony and a narrow outlook which is detrimental to your vision and achievement of ambitious career objectives.

Change in jobs leads to career diversification which results in broadening your perspective and outlook by gaining wide experience, expertise and knowledge in different streams and disciplines. Accepting such changes in jobs is always a noble and positive approach in building up your career and its advancement.

There are certain attributes such as drive, motivation, initiative, vision and urge which are required for enrichment of your life. They are responsible to cause you to move in that direction. Besides, your ambition acts like a motive power for driving you to achieve career advancement. As a result, you maintain your focus on searching different jobs which offer you better career prospects.

It is however advisable that you should settle down at some stage in one job or service in one organisation so as to have continuity, extensive utility and maximum contribution to that organisation by virtue of your longer service period. It also helps to gain sufficient seniority and proper standing in promotion and career advancement. What ultimately matters in promotions to senior and higher ranks and posts is your seniority, experience, maturity, knowledge and management skills. These parameters are used to assess your potential and abilities for making substantive and significant contribution to the organisation during your service period.

Career Advancement

It is a continuous process which basically involves personal development. Every organisation helps you by offering training programmes and courses. It is therefore your responsibility to take initiative, respond positively and show the positive results which are meticulously evaluated for the benefit of an organisation.

It is pointed out that career advancement is the responsibility of an individual who should take interest according to his goals, vision and ambition in order to attain higher ranks and status. The ladder of the career growth is fairly long and covers many stages, depending upon the rank structure of an organisation. As such, it is entirely up to you how you desire to rise and how much conscious you remain about your career advancement throughout your service period. Accordingly, your star and star plus attributes start playing an effective role and consequently influence your performance and achievement of the results thereof. It should however be remembered that not all Star and Star Plus attributes are required for promotion to junier and midle management levels. But, as you cross the middle stage of the growth ladder, more demands on your star and star plus attributes and lesser on negative attributes are placed and this becomes progressively more stringent for higher and top ranks. It is a fact that when you reach high or top position, it will certainly be the demonstration and consequence of your maximum Star and Star Plus attributes and the least influence of their negative ones. Both of them have effectively played their roles in causing your successive promotions thereby leading you to the higher and top positions.

Guidelines for Career Advancement (Mantras)

As a person grows up in rank and status, his self confidence and self-esteem start unknowingly swelling too. The feelings of too much of "self" that "I " am the achiever and main contributor start creeping in his mind. This phase of thinking too much about one self-especially when you start reaching fairly senior and higher levels of position is dangerous and likely to be counter productive if not checked well in time.

Hence, you are required to remain calm and cautious from two adverse factors firstly ego and secondly self-praise or brag. These two factors should be kept under control constantly and judiciously while you keep on making progress in achieving higher promotions and ranks in your organisation or industry. You may find a situation in which your subordinates may excite and praise you in your presence, reminding and eulogising about your achievements and contribution. At the same time, they may denigrate the top management. This is a crucial period of your career when you have to conduct yourself in a highly responsible and unassuming manner with due credit, being given to your subordinates as well as to the top management in in a loud and clear manner. You have to be tactful and diplomatic in your conduct and behaviour in order to demonstrate that your achievements and contribution could be possible due to the guidance and assistance from your seniors and top management from time to time. You have to state and appreciate assistance and cooperation of your subordinate staff in order to project a cohesive and harmonious team and its strong team spirit. You are the leader of this team and your assigned task is to deliver the goods with your total responsibility and accountability for the benefit of your organisation.

You are therefore advised to adopt the following steps as counseling mantras in case you desire to achieve higher career advancement in your organisation.

a) Control your ego and never allow it to appear in meetings, discussions and briefings.

b) Avoid self praise and the word "I" while stating or briefing about your activities. If this word "I" is replaced by "we", it is well received by your subordinates and seniors. At the same time, you should be judicious to use the word "I" where you wish to demonstrate to your top management about your exclusive role, responsibility and accountability.

c) Study the special attributes of your boss, background and his likes and dislikes. Find out his strong and weak points as well as the environment in which he is operating and also those whom he is reporting in the chain of command.

d) Accept always the authority and position of your boss and never try to override or overstep him, irrespective of his background, seniority and merit.

e) Since the power of expression is very important, express your views and points in clear, concise and forceful manner with due respect to your seniors if present there and with openness to connect them if they are found unfounded.

f) Learn the technique of selling to your management your concept, plan and perspective by following the principles of using precise, meaningful words and highlighting cost benefit factor with optimum employment of manpower and capital resources.

g) Be humble and polite but assertive and forceful in your objective presentation and participation with emphasis on organisational interest in your approach.

h) Be social and mingle with your selective group, team and friend circle. Never isolate yourself from the top management. Try to remain in limelight and within visible distance of the top management as much as possible without overdoing it.

i) Call on the boss and other members of the management with your family with prior appointment. Organise selective and occasion-based informal get-together or social events at your place.

j) Invite often the boss and other members of top management in the chain of reporting to your site or office and organise presentation and briefing for their information about your activities, responsibilities and resources and also the contribution being made by you and your staff. Introduce your staff and brief about their capabilities on such formal occasions so as to keep up their morale and sense of belonging and participation.

k) Organise a brainstorming session at least once in a month and discuss the subjects of organisation's interest. Encourage your subordinate staff to participate and express freely and frankly their views and opinion while you maintain a neutral position. Finally while summarising, give due credit to those who came out with positive and constructive proposals. Bring out such proposals along with your critical remarks and recommendations to the notice of the management.

l) Participate in lectures and brainstorming programmes of the top management voluntarily whenever called or arranged. Initiate dialog on issues and proposals of organisation's interest and keep them in limelight

m) Participate in the outdoor and indoor games whenever played by your boss and other senior members of the management in order to utilise such occasions for establishing personal contact and free interaction.

n) Never say that you are a busy person, thereby implying your openness and willingness to accept additional responsibilities and assignments.

o) Reminders for completing your jobs or assignments or submission of reports should be avoided or discouraged by completing them in time.

The steps or mantras as stated above are practical, rational, realistic and logical for the present competitive and challenging environment. These steps imply many attitudinal, functional and behavioral aspects of an individual who desires to step up the promotional ladder and attempts to reach fairly top positions as much as possible after placement and confirmation in a service. Several positive attributes are required to be present in a person. They do come out slowly and gradually act in a progressive manner during your upward transition over the growth ladder. At the same time, constant restraint and control has to be exercised on your negative attributes while remaining conscious about them.

Regular promotions and rise to higher ranks in your service period reveal presence of many valuable positive attributes in your nature, character, behaviour, personality and performance. The degree and level of their presence can be subjectively quantified as they vary over a considerable range. Their ranking and order of precedence also vary according to the size of an organisation and its corporate objectives.

It should be remembered that a good organisation always adopts universal techniques for discouraging ineffective, inefficient, unproductive and non-performing persons through the process of promotion of only the right persons in the progressive manner. Thus, only deserving and competent persons survive and keep getting promotions step by step. A few of them get to higher ranks but only one of them can reach the top position in the organisation at a point of time.

Management Techniques for Achieving High Level Career Advancement

In the present highly competitive environment, there is a mad rush and lust for going ahead and becoming superior in almost all fields, branches and faculties. This trend is found all over the world especially in the developed countries and it is also happening in the developing countries. While managing your service career under such difficult conditions with equally qualified people around in the competition, you are required to produce the result and maintain the lead in your career prospects. How is it possible? Here again, your personal qualities matter a lot and find manifestation in your nature, character, behaviour, abilities and performance. These can be harnessed in the form of special management techniques such as:

a) Achieve peak performance and try to establish professional edge over others.

b) Observe unwritten etiquettes, ethics, dignity and morality in behaviour, conduct and manners. Remain away from petty in-house politics

c) Maintain balance between work and home. Reduce your stress, strain and tension and maintain cheerful, joyful and composed posture and expression.

d) Always have an anchor or guru and maintain trust and confidence in him.

e) Manage cordial and amiable relationship with your boss in an obedient, respectful, responsive, dependable and dedicated manner without bothering about his seniority and professional competence.

f) Develop an effective network of well wishers and friends. Remain well-informed, well-versed, updated and maintain awareness, alertness about the environment around.

g) Learn to take risks and challenges with discretion and proper planning.

h) Increase your visibility by participating voluntarily in a lead role in seminars, group discussions, brainstorming sessions and always present your view-points, opinion forcefully without annoying others.

i) Understand thoroughly the policies, procedures, rules and objectives of the organisation / management. Learn to live with the realities on the ground without questioning since they are out of your control.

j) Be effective, meticulous, forceful and resounding in your communication by using proper words, sentences and pause for causing resonance and driving your viewpoint.

Caution and Warning

While managing your career, you need to guard against certain evils and immoral acts which are likely to spoil chances of your success that you have been meticulously achieving over the period. You will get a setback to your clean image and reputation. While you get progressive success and gain senior and high positions in your organisation, you are likely to overlook and neglect certain acts of basic values, morals and ethics. In fact, you should remain cautious on many fronts where you are likely to be waylaid and hijacked due to your temptation and certain weaknesses by your unscrupulous and selfish subordinates and middlemen. You should set for yourself a specific code of conduct. You should keep a watch around and never do anything hastily with a blind trust and faith. In fact, you should try to create a team of trustworthy, reliable and genuinely dependable subordinates with your discreet own watch and check mechanism and feedback network. Now, let us take a look at those evils and immoral acts which may unwittingly and unknowingly influence you in a negative manner.

a) Ego with a strong sense that you alone have done a great job thereby you are likely to get a false sense about yourself, belittling the role of others.

b) Self-pride (Abhiman) An excessive sense of Self esteem thereby getting a sense of superiority complex.

c) Flattery from your subordinates or certain selfish persons having vested interest.

d) Excessive self-confidence without any valid reason, basis and preparation.

e) Unsocial and unfriendly act of staying away from social functions, friends and relations.

f) Arrogance of power and authority.

g) Becoming much ambitious so as to lose sight of the realistic situation on the ground.

h) Neglecting close family members, friends and relations by saying that I am too busy.

i) Becoming autocratic while exercising command, control and supervisory functions.

j) Becoming a workaholic and ignore the sense of time management.

k) Unsympathetic and indifferent attitude towards the problems and issues of others.

Personality Factor

There is no doubt that impressive personality creates good impression and influence. A tall, handsome person with broad head and raised forehead makes impression. When he is smartly dressed and conducts himself in graceful and dignified manner, it creates favourable impression on others. Of course, these are physical body features and the disadvantage of not having such physical plus-points can be overcome if a person is genuinely efficient in his performance, loud and clear in expression and honest and sincere in delivering results. What ultimately matters is the end result, output and solid contribution. Even a person with short stature and moderate personality carries the audience with his oratory and powerful expression. Of course, proper dress, meticulous behaviour and graceful manners are definitely the factors, recognised for causing favourable impression. But it remains a short-term event and is no substitute for your effective, excellent performance, proper communication skills and deep professional knowledge.

Challenges of the twenty-first Century

You are already in this century and you have already started feeling the heat of it. What are those areas of challenges which you have to face in your service career and effectively manage for an honorable and dignified living. Let us take a look at those areas:

1. **Personal skills.** Your hard and soft skills demand continuous development, updating and upgradation due

to continuing changes in technology, operating procedures, competitive environment and globalisation. There is also threat to you from downsising of operations, market pressure and outsourcing. Simply having professional acumen and competence are not adequate. Much needed attributes such as tactfulness, diplomacy, soft expression, negotiating oral or written skill and personal and social touch should emerge from your soft skills.

2. **Good and effective communication.** You will have to be a good communicator in order to properly convey your thoughts, proposals, opinions and finally your expectations. You will have to receive feedback, understand fully its implications and ensure proper implementation in order to make certain the quantum and quality standards of the products and proper work culture.
3. **Teamwork.** Crossing of the boundaries in your responsibilities and functional roles can occur often with new structural changes in manpower and logistic supports. With the mixed and interactive nature of the jobs requiring multilateral support, you are actually working in an atmosphere of close-knit family with your team members, having close interactive and interdependent relationship in management areas of marketing, logistics, finances and manpower. Team work in such an environment is essential with the team spirit in order to produce the result.
4. **Visibility.** Others should be aware about your presence, abilities, potential and professional competence. They should see your performance and contribution. So, you have to move around, meet the people and discreetly apprise them about yourself. You have to remain open to new opportunities, concepts, ideas and absorb them expeditiously with the positive mindset.
5. **Well balanced life.** With increasing demand and pressure on your responsibilities and highly competitive environment around which is prone to produce stress, tension and mental agony, you need to devote your time and energy to your family, friends and relatives and thus

maintain a balance between your leisure pursuits and personal priorities. A well balanced life keeps you away from stress and tension and enhances your contributory potential and abilities.

6. **Expand your network.** As you want to advance your career and accomplish higher goals, you have to remain in touch with people of the mainstream and other streams as well. Your contact and close relationship with these people enable you to get timely information. advice, feedback, guidance, useful instruction and support. You should develop your acquaintances with a large spectrum of the people of different types and maintain it by sending greetings, congratulations, complements, invitations and occasionally writing letters and seeking their advice and blessings.
7. **Stay on the cutting professional edge.** You have to stay abreast of new developments in your professional field and also look around and acquire new ideas or modify your work style, methods, technique and change your goals accordingly.
8. **Conduct.** You should conduct yourself with absolute integrity, morality and uprightness and allow your reputation and image to spread around accordingly. That will enhance your moral character, strength, courage and temperament while dealing with the staff, subordinates and boss as well.
9. **Count every job**. You should maintain your interest and involvement in every job you choose or is assigned to you as additional responsibilities. It helps you while effecting change of job from one organisation to another or while trying to shift for diversifying your service assignments. The outcome of every job and the experience you get matters for your achievements and experience in the diversified fields of wide magnitude.

Role of Introspection in Career Management

Throughout the discussion so far on the subject of managing service career, you observe the emphasis on the personal qualities and how they play a significant role in different aspects of the service career. It becomes the moral duty of a person to do introspection and assess whether he possesses these qualities and if so, in what proportion and what are their synergy levels. At every stage, introspection plays its significant role in order to make a person aware about his power, strength and potential. It awakens him to feel the need to have necessary personal qualities in order to perform satisfactorily and meaningfully. After all, your fitness and suitability for promotions and undertaking higher responsibilities are being assessed on the basis of your performance and the results, you achieve.

Remember that it is the process of Introspection that makes you aware about your abilities, potential, talent, aptitude, attitude, mindset and habits. There is no other way of knowing about your Self unless somebody tells you after observing and monitoring your performance, nature and behavior. You may not like somebody telling you about your weak and negative points as it amounts to bluntly criticise you. It needs high moral and ethical courage and strength to receive and tolerate such criticism. So, the best way is for you to do introspection honestly and sincerely and ascertain your own positive and negative attributes and assess their proportions. Here, you are not giving a report to anyone, you are going to talk about them nor anybody has asked to know it. So, you get a fair and unbiased assessment about yourself in correct and pragmatic perspective. It enables you to become cautious, thoughtful and wise especially about your weak and negative qualities and induces you to take remedial measures for timely correction. You do not remain blind and unaware about the consequences and you can take the eventual failure and losses in good strides without becoming nervous, emotional and crestfallen. You develop a broad and mature vision to treat failure as the seed for future success. You also become broad minded for not entirely blaming others.

So, you have to appreciate the role of introspection in your service career where it directly and continuously helps you to effectively manage your career at various stages. You are also able to do your self-appraisal and find out your aptitude, attitude, talent, interest areas and finally assess your capability to withstand the competitive environment for placement and advancement. Introspection creates within you a sense for doing the right things for right purpose at right time and achieve your goals and objectives in the most productive and profitable way.

Thus, it is found that your Introspection and performance are so interrelated that they play the key roles in your service career. If you ignore introspection and go ahead with your performance, you will certainly do it but at your own risk. And time for any repentance and remorse would have gone past.

7

Introspection — A Positive Way to Understand Your Destiny

Scope

1. What is the nature of human destiny?
2. How is it correlated with your personal attributes?
3. What are the intermediate steps which are involved in this correlation process?
4. What is the role of luck factor?
5. What are the positive attributes for winning success?
6. What are the negative attributes for causing failure?
7. How effective is the role of introspection in unfolding secrets of the your destiny?

PRESENT SCENARIO

It is generally observed that you may have an ambition and strong desire to pursue your lofty goals and objectives but you can not achieve them and many times, you can't even make a meaningful start in that direction. You wish to become professional in one of your interest fields but you unwittingly and unwillingly land up in some profession in which you have the least interest and you would have never dreamt of it. You may have many mishaps, failures and losses in your missions and business. You may meet an accident and surprisingly survive with or without a scratch. In all these cases and incidents, there is a strong tendency to blame your destiny. This is a simple, standard, routine excuse and easiest escapist route from the reality for explaining your failure or non-achievement of your objectives in life. Whenever you analyse the reasons in such cases, you have invariably a tendency to blame the outside forces and so, you feign helplessness by saying that it was out of my control. Thus, you remain oblivious of the fact that your share of blame in such cases is the maximum but you try to evade accepting it yourself and unnecessarily bring the destiny in picture and overlook the reality. The basic issue gets thus stalled and sidetracked.

HUMAN DESTINY

Human destiny is a mystic aspect of your life. It is an imperceptible and invisible complex entity, having its roots in your beliefs, faiths, religion, philosophy, theology and spirituality. It is therefore deeply embedded in your mind, perceptions and feelings and comes forward to give you relief and solace from your failures and losses by giving the impression that the event was destined to happen and you had no control on it.

Hence, human destiny appears to be an abstract but incomprehensible complex entity. It implies occurrence of events with success or failure according to a certain predetermined schedule. It is presumed that it is already worked out and controlled by the divine forces. So, it remains much beyond your free will and control. Hence, it is believed that it is endowed to you at the time of your birth and you carry its imprint throughout your life. So, whatever happens in your life, its control mechanism lies in this imprint. It is thus projected as the super–natural invisible power which is supervising, guiding and controlling your life events. It is deemed to eventually become responsible for the end result of success or failure in your life. Consequently, it becomes a singular unique source for explaining the cause of a particular event in a convincing manner.

Destiny is also described as a purposeful, unexpected, unintended but focused march on a predetermined path which leads to your cherished goals and objectives which are your destination or conversely in your failure to reach there.

Since your destiny is endowed to you as a gift at the time of your birth by the heavenly forces in conjunction with the genetic factor contributed by your parents, it becomes a proper imprint of human personality and your brain-mind combination for operational-zing the lifelong activities and events. This is what you get from the cosmos as the heavenly gift of your destiny. To this, there is a contribution from the Mother Earth which offers you a place, shelter, environment, social surrounding, educational facilities, job and business opportunities and climatic conditions. These are counted as the Earth forces and it is your response to these forces that finally determines your gain or loss or success or failure in your life. Now, the questions raised are as under:

- What is the structure of this imprint?
- What does it constitute?
- Which part of your body does it control the most?

Although the human destiny is abstract and mystic, it still gives its individual response to the external agencies. Of course, it is quantitatively different and it significantly varies from person to person. It is this aspect that you have to discover because your destiny is an integral part of yourself.

It is seen that persons individually have different nature, character, potential, talent, abilities and personality. They behave, conduct and perform differently and at no time in an identical manner. So, their personal qualities of both positive and negative types substantially differ and consequently affect their personality and performance in a different manner. Since, success or failure depends upon your nature, character, behaviour, talent, skills and performance and since they are integrally related to your personal attributes or qualities, it is clear that your success or failure is basically correlated to your personal attributes which have dominance of either positive attributes or negative attributes or perhaps, both. With this correlation, having practically seen from our observations and experience, it is unequivocally possible to establish a close link of your destiny and personal attributes with the end result of success or failure in your life events and activities. In other words, your personal attributes play an important role in determining the end result and thus become the key factor for consideration between your destiny and success or failure in your service career. In this respect, you should remember that you are born with a different nature, temperament, intelligence, aptitude, personality, potential and abilities and you carry them within yourself as the heavenly gift in the form of an imprint of your identity and individuality since the day of your birth. It is the combination of the positive and negative qualities with variations in their strengths and relative levels that make a person different from one another. and consequently establishes his unique identity and existence. Hence, human destiny obviously gets dispensation in the basic combination of his inborn personal qualities and variations in their individual presence which constitutes personal attributes' profile with synergetic structuring.

To a common man, it is very difficult to understand and grasp the complex nature of this relationship between inborn personal qualities and his destiny. In fact, other side of the story reveals to us the events of failure or non-achievement of the lifelong goals as cases of lost opportunities. Numerous examples are found in cases of many persons for their losses or failures for reasons which appear to be out of their control. But after taking a close look and analysing the reasons honestly, truthfully and dispassionately, it is observed that most of the cases of lost opportunities are ultimately attributable to **personal qualities, especially of negative types such as indifference, casualness, selfishness, idleness, laziness, short-temperament, shortsightedness, narrow-mindedness, restlessness, short vision, etc**. These negative qualities adversely affect their nature, behaviour, character, skills, abilities and consequently their actual performance and relations in service career. Since, the direct responsibility here comes on you, it is commonly observed that you would not like to blame yourself nor you like anybody pointing the accusing finger at you. On the other hand, you pass the blame to the outside forces or you invariably make your destiny the scapegoat and pass the entire blame of the failure on your destiny. Here, the human intolerance, ego, ignorance and intransigence are responsible for him not to concede his failure and not to voluntarily accept his mistakes for taking remedial measures for correction. Thus, a case study of the lost opportunities enables you to take a close look at the real perspective of the destiny and its intimate relationship with your personal attributes especially those of negative types as stated above.

Correlation

Let us put the destiny as an abstract entity on one side and a set of personal attributes of both positive and negative types and their derivatives in different forms and combinations on the other side. Now, the question arises whether

These two entities are independent and exclusive.

Or

They are mutually interdependent.

Or

They are related to each other in some empirical form.

Or

They are simply correlated with each other.

After deeply deliberating on these issues and relationships as pointed out above, it is concluded that the destiny and personal attributes, although they appear to be two independent entities to our mind, are correlated to each other in an intrinsic manner. As a result, heavenly endowment of the personal attributes implies presence of the imprint of abstract destiny at the time of the birth which a child carries as a heavenly baggage for leading his service career and occurrence of all the life events. Once this aspect of relationship is clear, you get a reasonable, realistic and meaningful explanation for your success or failure as you get an opportunity to consider your personal attributes as the active agent of your destiny and its main actor. Once you start looking into your personal attributes on behalf of your destiny, you have partly unfolded the secret of your destiny.

It implies that these personal attributes as possessed by the human beings, are in fact mostly responsible for causing success or failure which is reflected in the form of gaining fortunes, prosperity, promotions, ranks, positions in your service career or failures and losses. Thus it can be boldly stated that:

- **Success is an indicator of the dominance of the positive attributes in you.**
- **Failure is an indicator of the dominance of the negative attributes in you.**

This is a simple way of looking at your success or failure and ascertaining its cause which eventually becomes attributable to yourself. In this respect, it is pointed out that dominant negative attributes significantly contribute to cause a failure or loss while dominant positive attributes cause success or boost the chances of success like your promotions and finally career advancement in your service career.

It is well known that the human destiny depends upon the time, date, month, year and place of the birth of a person. Astrologers give much credence to the birth data for preparing horoscope and determining human destiny. It is obvious that most of the personal attributes of positive and negative types are generated within a child in a differential manner at the time of its birth. Now, it is difficult to explain why and how the positive attributes dominate over the negative attributes or viceversa and in what manner their differential strengths and levels are set to occur. However, it can be logically and scientifically attributed to the genetic factor and presence of the cosmic forces, generated by different planets in their respective orbits along with the magnetic field of the earth, existing at the place of birth. Now, the personal attributes are broadly reflected in various functional domains such as mental, emotional, psychic, intellect and health. So, the genetic factor is generally considered responsible for imparting intellect, psyche and health while the cosmic factor is responsible for creating human mental and emotional structure with overlapping of the psychic elements. Remember that it is very broad and general classification of personal attributes in different functional domains. Their contributory factors have tremendous power and potential for making differential contributions and establishing different identities in human beings.

Interconnectedness of Personal Attributes

It has been stated that human destiny and personal attributes are correlated with each other. Now, the question is, how? **What is the mechanism of interconnectedness? What is its profile?** This intra-relationship is illustrated step by step in the subsequent paragraphs.

Step 1

Personal attributes of both positive and negative types affect your mindset, habits, manners, style, attitude, temperament and body movements.

Step 2

These features of your personality determine your nature, character, abilities, potential, and conduct.

Step 3

They in turn influence your performance, behaviour, activities, functioning, relationship, learning and updating of your professional skills.

Step 4

It naturally leads to achievements, results, accomplishments, success.

Step 5

These factors are of course based on evaluation and assessment of your quality, eligibility, acceptability and utility.

Step 6

It is now after completion of this step and suitably reporting confidentially that you are considered for progressive promotions, higher appointments, ranks, status, awards, recognition.

Step 7

These achievements are your normal Aspirations and are direct fruits of your favourable destiny.

Profile of your destiny

This is one way of looking at the profile of your Destiny. You can look on this correlation of intra relations from another angle of taking the Destiny as the starting point of your lifelong gift and anticipate its direct offshoots and consequences on successive events of your service career. This particular aspect with a different approach is illustrated as under:

Step 1

Your normal aspirations from your destiny are wealth, fortune, progressive promotions to higher ranks, status, awards, recognition and prosperity.

Step 2

They depend upon your eligibility, suitability, qualifications and utility.

Step 3

These aspects are determined by evaluation, assessment and Appreciation of your results, achievements and accomplishment

Step 4

But, they depend upon your performance, activities, deeds, relationship, behaviour, learning and updating of your professional skill.

Step 5

These are directly affected by your nature, character, abilities, potential, and conduct.

Step 6

Which depend upon your mindset, habits, manners, style, attitude, body movements and temperament.

Step 7

They are in turn determined by your personal qualities of both positive and negative types.

It is observed that there are a number of intermediate stages; a person has got to go through for ultimately becoming eligible for getting the desired and cherished fruits of his destiny in the form of wealth, fortune, prosperity, promotions, high status, recognition etc. which are known as the aspirations of the human beings. At every stage, there is an assessment and evaluation of your performance. This is a continuous process which is elaborate and properly structured. A person receives promotions and awards only after he has gone through this entire process and receives due recommendations from his superior officers. Thus, the fruits of your destiny do fall in your hands but only after you work hard, struggle intelligently and perform in such a manner that it comes to the notice and is recognised, approved and valued by your senior officials.

This sequence of steps which depicts intermediate events invariably takes place in any organisation. It is a normal procedural process and final result is seen only after the end of the complete process. A person who has reached upper class of positions has invariably achieved progressive promotions and has gone through these intermediate stages in his service tenure. A person who has reached the top position in any organisation is called a highly lucky person but before that he has gone through the rigorous process, delivered the goods and substantially contributed to his organisation. So merely calling him lucky is to grossly underestimate his skills, talent, abilities and potential which he has actually demonstrated in his performance through his personal attributes especially positive types which have played dominant role in his performance. Thus, outstanding performance becomes the true indicator of his dominant positive attributes which produce impact and effective influence at every stage. Besides, such persons are able to avail and utilise right opportunities at right times and adopt a systematic approach without getting confused or misguided. They do not deviate from their mission path but go all out for achievement of their lifelong objectives. They have their mission clear in their vision and proceed with strong will power, tenacity, drive and motivation. They have firm determination and commitment to adhere to their short as well as long term objectives.

Luck Factor

To understand clearly the human luck factor which is generally and loosely talked about, you must firstly remember and appreciate that it is always linked with right opportunities and right time for occurrence of a particular event like service interviews, vacancies, professional courses, training workshops, appointments, proper friends, marriage, etc. They do occur with prior notice and announcement. Now, it is you who has to take note of such incoming events. A person whenever he avails such an opportunity is guided by his drive, motivation, initiative and vision for grabbing it. He would also like to put in his honest, sincere and dedicated efforts which involve his hard work, struggle, perseverance, determination, commitment and patience. Persons, having such attributes are creative and possess remarkable abilities, competence, potential and amiable nature with high ethical values. In other words, it is basically possession of the Star qualities and their manifestation in candidates which eventually become responsible for them to push and avail such opportunities and subsequently demonstrate them in their performance at right times on right occasions. In fact, it is the combination of Star and Star Plus qualities as possessed by the candidates that eventually make them eligible for achieving positive results and success at various stages of their service careers. People who talk so loosely about the luck factor should sincerely do introspection and ascertain where they stand as compared to those so called lucky persons who have gone up to the higher and top positions in their respective organisations.

Of course, there appears to be a strong correlation between the luck factor and personal star attributes. In fact, such a luck factor is critically perceived in persons who are found to possess awareness, responsiveness, time consciousness and vision for their career. As a result, they are spontaneously driven, motivated and guided to act and move in the direction where they are likely to have positive success in their undertakings and missions. It is obvious that those who do not possess the above qualities will certainly fail to take proper cognisance of the opportunities and eventually miss them for ever. Besides, they are likely to face failures in their service careers. This critical observation significantly leads to the correlation of the failure or loss with the negative star qualities which functionally dominate in such persons.

There may be some illogical belief that the success or failure of such persons is associated with the past deeds of their own or their parents who might have performed in their previous births or past life. This belief may be partly true in the sense that a few of the personal attributes as stated earlier are genetically passed on to a child from their parents. Of course, these are modified to a certain extent under the influence of the cosmic and earthly forces as present at the time of its birth. Such persons are likely to be positively or negatively influenced during their upbringing and academic period by the environmental, socio-economic and geopolitical structure and their corresponding good or evil forces.

Effective Role of Introspection

It is now definitely clear that the process of introspection plays a very important role not only in revealing many features and characteristics of your personality but also in helping you to control and correct your important negative and undesirable attributes which affect your performance and relations. You come to know about your personal qualities of both positive and negative types and their influence on your daily activities, functioning and performance. Your final success or failure mainly depends upon the dominating aspect of positive or negative attributes because they basically determine your nature, character, mindset, behaviour, relationship, habits, conduct and performance. They also affect your upbringing, education, abilities, work culture, training and professional uptake level. Your professional skills and organising and managing techniques depend upon another set of personal attributes such as responsiveness, comprehension, assimilation, willingness, attentiveness and flexible attitude. They come to play a very significant role while you are attending training classes, workshops, tutorials and seminars for updating your knowledge and professional skills. Consequently, your progressive promotions to higher ranks and status are determined by the quality and grade of your performance and achievements thereof.

The only way for you to discover your personal attributes is by adopting the technique of Introspection for which you should set aside some time from your busy schedule and devote yourself for seriously peeping within yourself. In this process, you deeply deliberate on yourself by looking within and directly start addressing introspective queries to yourself and try to seek answers honestly, sincerely and truthfully. Thus, you discover the treasure of your positive and negative qualities and eventually become aware about your hidden source of immense energy, potential and capacity for giving you strength, courage, boldness, firmness, endurance and confidence. At the same time, you become aware about your weaknesses on account of your negative attributes such as anger, laziness, casualness, selfishness, indifferent attitude, greed, dishonesty, etc. As a result, you are in a position to assess your nature, character, mindset, talent, attitude, potential as well as your temperamental short comings and weak points on account of possessing certain star negative qualities and ascertain if they exceed tolerable specified limits. You also come to know about the strong points of your personality on which you can capitalise and exploit them to the fullest extent in your performance. They also help you in facing risks and challenges in your service career thereby placing you ahead of others in the competitive race.

Once, you know about your attribute profile and about the dominance of either positive or negative types, you can try to strengthen those attributes which you need the most in your specific career and associated performance and control those which are likely to retard your performance and create setbacks in the career. Remember that whenever you successfully go through many hurdles, problems, difficulties and adverse conditions and still finally achieve your objectives and goals, then the credit should basically go to your positive attributes which have enabled you to steer through successfully. This is the appropriate time for you to look back and find out those specific positive attributes which are present within you. But, instead of doing this objective work, you try to attribute your success and achievement to your destiny. In fact, it is basically you and your treasure of certain positive attributes which have pulled you out and placed you on the pedestal of success for which you unwittingly give credit to your destiny. In a way, you find that your destiny rests with you and is an integral part of yourself. Consequently, success or failure in your service career becomes your own function and exclusive responsibility.

Positive Attributes for Winning Success

Now, let us take a look at those important personal positive attributes which substantially contribute in enabling you to achieve your career oriented objectives and take you to your destination. They basically belong to the treasure of your hidden and latent positive qualities which come in action and drive you to perform successfully. These are listed below:

1. **Adaptability**—To any situation, conditions, environment, staff, boss.
2. **Commitment**—To your organisation and given or assigned tasks and objectives.
3. **Confidence** — Trust in yourself that you will execute the work successfully.
4. **Dedication** — To concentrate your attention and energies on the given task.
5. **Dependability**—Your credibility and truthfulness as perceived by your boss or organisation.
6. **Integrity and loyalty**—Pertains to your moral attachment, trust, belonging and faithfulness.
7. **Knowledge**—Learning and training for acquiring new skills and updating existing skills, pertaining to your profession, organisation and management. Required for high positions and senior appointments and enables you to gain promotions. A totally voluntary act.
8. **Mountain mover**—Means a person having tremendous seal, drive, initiative, stamina, enthusiasm, keenness and motivation. He goes all out for achievement with full force, energy and high spirit.
9. **Patience, politeness and humbleness**—It means to wait for proper opportunity and then strike. Related to your behaviour and conduct.
10. **Communication skill**—Pertains to your expression verbally and in writing for making contact with others and to explain your views and opinion.
11. **Responsiveness**—Pertains to your capacity and reaction for absorbing training and gaining knowledge. Indicates your vigilance, attentiveness and assimilation.

12. **Talent**—Pertains to your intellect and IQ level.
13. **Vision**—Capacity to look beyond the horizon and visualise your long term objectives and mission.
14. **Willingness**—It is readiness to undertake responsibilities and work of your own.
15. **Urge**—A driving force of your inner Self to achieve a particular objective.

These are selected specific positive attributes which are key players and strong indicators of your favorable destiny. They exercise positive influence on your personality and performance and lead you to win positive success in your life.

Negative Attributes that cause Failure

Now, let us take a look at important negative qualities / attributes which affect your mind and result into your bad temper, relations, behavior and conduct. They adversely influence your thought process and divert in the wrong direction. As a result, your personality, performance and relations badly suffer. Consequently, bad and adverse impression and opinion are created about you in office and public. This proves to be quite damaging to your career and so to your destiny. Most of these negative attributes are inborn and some of them become evident at young age and some erupt at later stages of life as you grow. During this interim period, some of these attributes remain hidden deep in mind and come out later at unforeseen and unpredictable times. These are listed below:

1. **Anger**—Related to loosing temper and getting into rage, sometimes becoming violent and wild.
2. **Aggressiveness**—Readiness to attack or quarrel.
3. **Carelessness and casualness**—Not being attentive and lacking in self- management.
4. **Craziness**—Irrational fondness and foolishness.
5. **Dominance** –Feeling a sense of superiority and riding high on it.
6. **Egotism**—Selfish thinking and talking much or boasting about self and own achievements only.
7. **Greediness and selfishness**—Keeping self interest above all and tendency to grab.

8. **Impulsiveness**—Urge or sudden action without thinking.
9. **Indifference**—Showing no interest in jobs, relations and performance.
10. **Introvert**—Looking inwards to yourself, sticking to personal viewpoints and opinion.
11. **Possessiveness**–Excessive sense of possessing without respecting other's claim.
12. **Rigidity**—Holding to personal views right or wrong and not bending or yielding.
13. **Rudeness**—Showing bad manners and impolite behaviour.
14. **Stubbornness**—Unwilling to give way and difficult to manage.
15. **Temperamental**—Becoming excited and moody on slightest impulse or stimulus.
16. **Sexiness**—Getting highly excited on sex matters.

These are prominent negative personal attributes which adversely affect your mind and drive it to think in the wrong direction. They become the adverse key players in causing your bad or unfavorable destiny because they will stand as obstacles and oppose the way to your destination. Obviously, it will cause failure in achievement of your mission and lifelong objectives.

It is thus seen that these personal positive and negative attributes become fairly good indicators of your destiny and whether they should result in good or bad destiny depends upon the dominance of concerned positive or negative attributes.

Concluding Remarks

While concluding this chapter, it is observed that the process of Introspection has a significant and meaningful role in determining your destiny, particularly related to your service career. The fact is that your performance is dependant on your nature, character, behavior, mindset, intellect and relations. So, your personal attributes of both positive and negative types become major contributory factors in enabling to march towards your destiny and achieve its fruits such as fortune, wealth, promotions, status and prosperity. You have already taken a close look at the intermediate stages which you have got to go through so as to become entitled for promotions and advancement in your service career.

When this is the real factual situation on ground, it is surprising why you people do not seriously take cognisance of your self-introspect process. There is always the excuse that you don't find time to devote to yourself. You feel that you are so busy that you can't ponder about yourself. You always engage in loose talking about introspection without being serious to actually implement it in a systematic manner. It is perhaps due to the human apprehension that this process may reveal some negative bad points about you. And the human nature is such that it does not accept anything bad about him. He may commit the mistakes but he will not like to morally accept and openly own up the mistakes. Personal ego and high sense of self-esteem try to override your willingness to admit. This is human psychology and you have to get over it for winning real success in life.

This explains why Introspection is not popular and people are reluctant to do it. Its real reason lies in the human psychology that you can never be wrong and can no commit mistakes. The day you overcome this psychological barrier; you become open-minded and flexible in your attitude. As a result, you open the gate to your destiny. How far, you go is a matter of conjecture but it certainly means that you have taken the first important step in your career. Once you keep in mind the correlation of your personal attributes with your destiny and remain aware and conscious about it at every stage of your service career, you are certain to take the next step to proceed in your career in a positive and optimistic manner that enables you to avoid frustration, disappointment and disillusionment in life and maintain calm and composed posture.

This is the beginning of your getting awakened to the reality and becoming enlightened in your life. You will see more of this aspect in the next chapter.

8

Self-Awakening and Enlightenment through Introspection

SCOPE

1. **How do you approach for understanding the subject?**
2. **What are the risks and challenges in your life?**
3. **What do you mean by an awakening stage?**
4. **What is the technique for self-awakening?**
5. **How do you come to know about yourself?**
6. **How do you know about your destiny through the self- awakening process?**
7. **What are the practical aspects of self-enlightenment?**

Approach

While discussing the role of introspection in self-awakening and enlightenment, it appears that you are entering the philosophical and spiritual aspects of your life. You are somehow trying to dabble and know something which is much beyond the common man's comprehension and general understanding because it pertains to upper level of mystic knowledge and theosophical understanding. It may not concern you in your day-to-day life and you may not even feel its impact on your normal functioning because you remain concerned and engrossed in satisfying your basic needs and aspirations. But, those who have achieved their material objectives like wealth, fortunes, promotions, status and all round prosperity, do feel some vacuum in their life and have shown urge and longing for achieving something by which they can really feel mental happiness, peace and contentment. These mental needs have nothing to do with your material achievements but they belong to the inner part of your Self. Some call them the longing of your soul or some call them the urge of your spiritual Self, some see in them the happiness of the highest mental level. This may be called your enlightened stage where you have gained the knowledge, wisdom, maturity, devotion, reverence and detachment. At this stage, you fearlessly see the world with no boundaries, no horizon with infinite spread and full of pure, selfless, divine love which happens to be beautifully connected with your life. With the wisdom and knowledge that you gain in the process, you see no dark side, no negative aspect, no fear, no anger, no resentment, no temptations and no attachment with your material life and relations.

Well, I have talked of a very high state of your mind which has to be lifted up from its embedded beliefs, traditions, practices and worldly attachment called temptation which means *moha* and *maya jal* in Hindi language. All those cobwebs belonging to the earthly material life have to be cleared by the real knowledge, wisdom, vision, prayers, meditation and deep spiritual growth in order to reach that high level of the platform which pertains to the higher reaches of your inner Self and personal life.

Human Life

Human life is not a bed of roses. It passes through high levels of ups and downs. The path to your destination is not straight and it has ditches, turns, bends, slopes and up-hills. As a result, your life undergoes through innumerable sufferings of various types with some periods of pleasure, delight, happiness and satisfaction. With such a human life you have inherited in endowment since your birth, you have to bear and live with it. Obviously, you should look for some natural remedial measures which can really uplift you from the morasses of negatives and darkness and swing you to the other side of light, hope and relief. Now the questions are:

- **How to do it?**
- **How are you going to mend your flaws and correct your negatives?**
- **How are you going to recover from the wounds, inflicted by your sufferings and failures?**

Efforts are made for seeking answers to the above questions in the subsequent paragraphs.

Challenges and Risks

Challenges and risks are an integral part of your life. They open out glorious opportunities for personal growth and positive transformation and enable you to reach out to your cherished objectives. While doing so, they demand that you demonstrate enough courage, boldness, moral strength, motivation, perseverance and foresight in order to face and overcome them with careful planning and thoughtful action. These are important personal attributes of your nature and character and they come up for action from deep within yourself. As such, whenever a challenging situation arises and you boldly face and overcome it, it becomes your awakened appearance where you have lifted yourself to a high moral, courageous, fearless and powerful level thereby causing a transformation within yourself by activating your hidden faculties for playing an effective role in your life on such crucial occasions.

Awakening Stage

As you look at the issue, there are two types of the awakening state. One is philosophical and spiritual type and as such it belongs to the upper level of your life which is not commonly comprehensible to a common man. The other type belongs to yourself from the career point of view. While the former type of awakening deals with your soul and other metaphysical, theological and cosmic aspects which one likes to know for lifting himself from the material earthly belongings and get freed from the chain of birth, the latter part assumes importance and relevance from practical point of view as it helps you in causing your Self-development and managing your personality and career. Actually, this part brings for you the material benefits like wealth, fortune, promotions and prosperity. I would like to deal with this latter part as it concerns your personal career and life.

Human Life Pattern

As a child grows and attains his adolescence and adulthood, he remains largely oblivious about himself and his capabilities and potential. At what stage he starts realising his potential and abilities and how it happens are not precisely known even to his parents. It is also not known whether he makes any serious and sincere efforts to know about himself. He maintains his normal routine, makes random choices, has a hit and miss approach and conducts himself most of the time according to his whims, fancies and external forces. Parents do play a significant role in shaping their children's career. While the process of personal growth is on, nobody including their parents remain aware about the need for initiating the process of self-awakening within them. Of course, they have to become active and dynamic persons and effectively demonstrate self-confidence, self-awareness, self-esteem and self-honour. But, if a person does not know about himself, how is he going to demonstrate such qualities which help him to establish his identity and stamp his personality? So, you should be aware of the following two aspects:

a) Self-demonstrating qualities related to your inner Self and reflected into your self-confidence, self-awareness, self-esteem, self-honour and self-responsiveness.

b) Need to establish your individual identity and stamp your personality by your nature, relations, behaviour, conduct, skill and performance.

It is obvious that the second part depends on the first part and it is enough to tackle this part in order to reach the second part.

Technique for Self-Awakening

The technique which I would like to highlight is to adopt a Self-Awakening Mission which includes a process of self-questioning and searching for appropriate answers. This self-questioning is addressed to yourself and can be about the following

a) Know the birth environment, status of parents, family background, your personality, behaviour, habits, manners, and health. Think about your physical status, behavioural pattern and habits.

b) Know about your working style, performance and communication skills oral and written.

c) Think about your studies and academic performance at primary, secondary and college levels.

d) Think about the type and nature of dialog and communication you have with your parents, teachers and about thé extent of their advice and guidance in your studies.

e) Find out your aptitude, liking, interest, involvement and commitment.

f) Ascertain your consciousness and awareness about the career, setting lifelong mission and seriousness and will power for achieving your aspirations.

g) Think about your hobbies, pursuits, tastes and how you spend your spare time.

h) Find out your religious bent of mind, approach to divine powers, visit to worshiping places, interest in religious and philosophical subjects, prayers, faith in rituals and traditions. Is your faith lasting or occasional?

You can have your own mechanism in the form of working out a schedule of questions and then addressing them to yourself under the above groupings heads and find out the honest and truthful answers. Once, you are ready with true personal information and data, you come to know about your real nature, behaviour, talent, potential, abilities, skills and physical status such as health, stamina, endurance and body features and body language from your habits and manners. You will be surprised to know such information and rediscover yourself that it will generate awareness and confidence about your strengths and weaknesses and you will realise how to control and correct the negative qualities such as anger, greed, ego, casualness etc. Broadly, you come to know from such an exercise information about yourself as under:

a) The level of your stamina, endurance, capacity, tenacity and tolerance. It makes you health conscious.

b) Mental and emotional strength, weakness and need to control and correct weakness.

c) Special features of your physic and personality such as pointed nose, broad forehead, big eyes, typical body movements, style of walk, standing and manners of speaking and listening.

d) Level of your talent, IQ, intellect and studious nature from your academic performance and grades obtained in various examinations.

e) Team spirit, leadership, cooperation, comradeship, coordination and discipline.

f) Level of your general knowledge and current affairs if you have the habit of reading books and newspapers. Also about your creative and artistic mind if you are following certain hobbies.

g) Positive mindset when you have an optimistic and constructive approach to your work.

h) Self-driven, responsive, dependable and motivated person when you willingly work, accept additional responsibilities, take initiatives and complete the task and assignment within the given time schedule.

i) Urge and quest for learning and gaining knowledge when you read books, magazines and visit libraries.

j) Humbleness, politeness and nobility when you respect teachers, parents and feel a deep sense of gratitude for those who help you.

k) Social, caring with loving nature and mutual respect when you have close friends and when you participate in social functions and activities.

l) Daring, courageous and adventurous attitude when you do riding, hiking, swimming and rock climbing.

m) Eco-friendliness and nature loving when you care for nature, animals, plants and do gardening.

n) Good organising and managing skills when you organise functions, execute events and conduct reality shows.

o) Independent bent of mind when you work with your own hands and need no supervision / spoon feeding.

These are enough indicators and marking events which activate a state of social, academic, interactive, intelligent and behavioural awakening and transformation in you. It enables you to know where you stand, about your position and how you react. It is sort of a social and intelligent engineering which causes a revolution within you and makes you enlightened about yourself. Imagine that you don't act and remain quiet without taking any action on the above stated lines. In that case, you are likely to remain ignorant about your potential, strength, weakness, aptitude, attitude, mindset and interest areas. Suppose, you are doing well and achieve success in coming up by overcoming difficulties and hardships. Do you have a reasonable explanation for your success? Of course, your personal qualities will indirectly and unknowingly drive you to deliver good performance and have good behaviour and relations. But, the fact prevails that you remain oblivious about your own power and strength and perform without any knowledge about yourself. Although you have achieved success, you would have realised that you didn't have in your entire operation proper spirit, force, drive, confidence and moral strength which would have otherwise made significant difference to your activities by virtue of becoming self-awakened. In case of the failures, you would have certainly known about your weak points that should have apprised you about the causes and forewarned you to take appropriate remedial meassures.

Destiny through the Self-Awakening Process

There are some people who believe that human destiny occurs through the process of self-awakening. As this process unfolds and reveals many important human positive attributes, it definitely lays the foundation and indicates the glorified future. These people believe that once you possess these qualities, the destiny will certainly call on you. Only, the need exists that you must be strict, truthful and honest to yourself while going through the process of self-awakening as listed above and doing your real assessment. Here, this process enables you to establish connection to your Self and initiate the action of "Know Thyself". Follow the theme of "Know Thyself and Your Destiny will discover You".

In the pursuit of your destiny, self-awakening is identified as the process of self- discovery which has strong potential to add enormous values and enrichment to your life and career. You definitely get direction and momentum in your actions and movements as you are able to tread safely and boldly with knowledge, wisdom, courage and foresight. It also reveals to you the possibilities of abundant choices in service careers that should suit to your abilities, aptitude and temperament. In the process, you come to know certain universal truths and natural laws that govern the world. Once, you align your life schedule with the natural laws, you realise the force of your personal spirit, fire and brilliance which open the vistas of your destiny with the self-control mechanism for establishing balanced work schedule, career and living. This is how you discover a way of understanding how life works and what is the right thing for you. Thus, you get a golden opportunity to discover various facets of your life in order to reach your destiny.

Self-awakening is a remarkably potent process for conducting your real living with the positive approach and mindset and full awareness about the environment that leads you towards your destiny. It manifests your inherent power and potential with which you have come into this world. It reveals all your beliefs, fears, assumptions, values along with dominating positive and negative qualities and their respective force levels. Thus, self-awakening becomes the first step to evaluate heights of your personal greatness and glory by offering you certain essential practices for integrating into your life. It eventually becomes an exercise to awaken the brain-mind-body combination for exploring your core beliefs, apprehensions, inhibitions and assumptions that generally create setbacks in the path to your favourable destiny. It is possible to overcome them by learning, patient listening and acquiring knowledge and wisdom. This is the intelligent work and manner which enable you to acquire moral strength and courage for advancing on the moral and spiritual path and learn the mechanism for controlling your emotions, passions, feelings, temperament and negative thoughts.

Along with the awakening of mind, there is the need to awaken your body too so that **healthy mind rests within the health body**. It reflects positive and productive integral combination of both mind and body. In this respect, you are advised to do regular exercises, meditation, yoga and observe healthy habits of diet and stay away from vices. In such a process where awakening of both mind and body takes place together, it reflects into initiating positive action for accomplishing favourable destiny. It certainly indicates your right step in the right direction.

Spiritual Approach

So far, you have seen the practical aspects and you can realise its impact on your life and service career. Of course, this is very important as you have to live, survive and achieve your material objectives. It is only after satisfying material needs that you will be able to think of the spiritual need which becomes the next stage for achieving real peace, happiness and satisfaction in whatever you have so far gained. In fact, it entirely depends upon you how you are able to use and dovetail the knowledge, wisdom and experience from your first stage of awakening into this stage of spiritual awakening.

Of course, it is a difficult stage and you may have to refer to the books on philosophy, theology, spirituality and religion and discreetly pick up information and advice which should become relevant to your purpose.

Spiritual awakening offers to you a code of conduct and ethical, moral approach with emphasis on values, principles and morality. In philosophical and spiritual approach, you come to know many seasons of your life with variations in hardships and pleasantness. However, they do not last for ever and they follow the cyclic order in their occurrences. It is your intense desire and tremendous hope that enable you to pull out from the storms whenever they occur and help you reach your destination. Here, you should remember that you grow taller from your sufferings and handicapps by your intense grit, determination, courage, ambition and vision. It creates within you the intense fire and will power to overcome the sufferings which you strongly feel that they are temporary and will not last for long. Eventually, you are not afraid of a failure which you take in a good stride and spirit. In fact, you try to learn from the mistakes in a pragmatic manner. Whenever the tough and adverse time and situation occur, you keep your mind, body, emotions and spirit in proper operating order. Your finely tuned mental condition encourages you to take risks and face them boldly and courageously. Finally, you come to know that you are not alone and there are many with you and they look up to you for leadership and guidance for steering them from their difficult conditions.

It is finally observed that self-awakening makes you a different, knowledgeable, wise, empowered person with a broad mindset. You start looking at your life and service career from a positive and pragmatic angle with optimistic vision for growth, development and expansion allround. It now leads to the next phase i.e. Enlightenment.

Enlightenment

The field of enlightenment basically pertains to the spiritual domain where the seers and religious saints talk of relief and escape from the chain of the birth and rebirth, called *Moksha* in Hindi language. It also means to know the true meaning of human life and controlling divine power of the cosmos. Finally, it amounts to accept the supreme power and authority of the God over human life. Thus, such a perception and realisation leads to utmost knowledge and remarkable wisdom which cause redemption of your inner Self and Soul. Such a state is called enlightenment where you feel a sense of fire, upsurge and divine spirit within your Self. You are thus lifted up above the earthly belongings, temptations and common vices and placed at a fairly high level in wisdom and knowledge, compared to a common man. It is possible for you to achieve such a state with your dedicated worship, prayers, deep meditation, sacrifices of material comforts, simple living and high level thinking for global care and welfare.

Well, such an enlightened state remains mystic to young people who believe in its practical and physical aspects and applications. They look for such practices and methods that can make them enlightened from practical point of view and become useful in their service careers for achieving success. It means that they would like to have the specific enlightenment that will help them to achieve material benefits for living comfortably and enjoying their life. As a result, the entire conventional concept of enlightenment gets a different dimension in the modern context.

Practical Aspects of Enlightenment

When you are set on your career path, you have to observe certain guidelines and code of conduct for yourself. Your life has to be governed by certain rules and principles in order to enable you to stay within certain moral and ethical boundaries. In other words, you should follow certain values, principles, ethics, etiquettes and code of conduct in your work, performance, behaviour and relations. At the same time, you should realise the importance of learning and improving your knowledge and keeping yourself informed on all fronts. Once you follow values and principles and you have sufficient knowledge of philosophy, spirituality and religion besides that of your profession, you get charged up certain spirit and sense a fire for spiritual upliftment. You do not deviate from just, moral and noble path. You get a different type of wisdom, outlook and vision where you start giving more importance to the humanity, morality, nobleness and generosity. Eventually, it creates within you the spirit of commitment, involvement and dedication that make you more responsible, accountable, committed person while discharging your duties, obligations and assignments.

Hence, once you are awakened, the next step leads you to enlightenment through the process of actions as listed above. You start feeling yourself a different person with your high morale and spirit lifted up. Your outlook becomes broad, positive and pragmatic with intense passion created for seeking upliftment in knowledge, wisdom, prayers and meditation. You start feeling differently with a sense of detachment from material prosperity but attachment to morality, nobleness, dignity and generosity. In the process, you stay away from vices, bad habits, negative mindset and selfish attitude.

CAUTION

It is advised that while you are set on the path of enlightenment, you should remain aware and conscious of your commitments and obligations to your career and its objectives. Enlightenment does not mean running away from your basic duties, obligations and responsibilities but it is your sincere and honest effort to lead a peaceful, happy and contended life which should be free from stress, tension, fear, suspicion, envy, greed and frustration. It should also enhance the standard and quality of your living with human approach in your relations and conduct. It should really make you a knowledgeable, wise and noble person with dignified manners, disposition and rich thoughts. You will eventually remain cheerful and maintain calm and composted posture while boldly facing risks and challenges in your life.

So finally, it is highly important to know and observe that enlightenment brings a transformation in you and creates remarkable spirit and fire within you whereby you gain moral strength, power, forbearance and peace of mind with mental happiness and prosperity. This is definitely a positive march to your true destiny.

9

Becoming an Achiever through Introspection

SCOPE

1. What is the profile of your achievement?
2. What types of odds and adversities occur in the life of an achiever?
3. What do you mean by handicap level and trade off?
4. How does introspection play the role in this respect?
5. What are the words of wisdom that you should follow as guidelines?
6. What is the positive attitude of an achiever?
7. What do you mean by extra-factor or plus-factor?
8. What is the role of talent in the life of an achiever?

Profile of Achievements

If you want to be an achiever, then let it be in whatever field of your choice. Your field may be big or small but it indicates your intense desire and interest to proceed and pursue a particular field with zeal, thrill and commitment. You may be alone or receive support and patronage from some well-wishers or get their blessings. With that moral strength, support and direction, your inner spirit will be fired and driven in the right direction. You will gain momentum in order to face and overcome obstacles, bends and turning on your life path. You will finally reach your destination where you will rejoice and celebrate the successful achievement of your cherished objectives. Those who listen to the voice of their inner Self and tune their energies and spirit in consonance with the working environment and people around will sense a signal from their destiny. As a result, they will drive themselves with full inner force, potential and strength towards the accomplishment of the goals and mission of their life. This activism and courage with single minded attention, decision and complete devotion magnificently stand high on the pedestal of their destiny. Consequently, they are encouraged and motivated to go all out after their objectives and accomplish them. Thus, they finally become the achievers in their life.

Meaning and Rider

So far, it sounds like receiving a philosophical message and advice since it has addressed to the imperceptible inner forces, potential and other factors that stand behind an achiever.

What does it mean to be an Achiever?

It simply means that you achieve with hard work something which you dream and earnestly wish to finally accomplish and be fully satisfied. Now, there is a rider applied in respect of such achievers. It means that their achievements are against the backdrop of the most adverse, difficult, uncongenial and unfavourable conditions and circumstances. A person with smooth sailing and having faced no problems and difficulties of any nature is not classified as an achiever or is not entitled to be called an achiever because he gains the things in a natural way where there was no struggle, hard work, competition and combative environment. Hence, in an achiever, what is hidden is the intensive struggle and pursuit against heavy odds and adverse conditions. That is why his final achievement entitles him to be called a true achiever in its real sense. The adverse conditions, severe struggle and pursuit of final achievement go together. At every stage, willpower, abilities, potential and moral strength of a person is subjected to intensive tests and he is required to overcome his despair, disappointment and depression on occurrence of any unpleasant event or failure or loss while pursuing his objective. His personal qualities such as determination, firmness and indomitable courage along with his capacity to work hard with perseverance and endurance are often put to severe test. The whole process appears to be an exercise of walking through fire with imminent threat of burning and getting bruises if you do not carefully maneuver and manage to safely come out. If you are able to come out, you become an achiever.

So, while looking into the meaning of an achiever, you are constantly reminded of the extreme odds and adverse conditions and circumstances surrounding a person in which he is deeply embedded since his childhood. His struggle, endurance and high spirit enable him to come out of these morasses and overcome the initial handicap level. This process reveals his high moral strength, courage and indomitable spirit for fighting and moving forward on the path of his objectives and goals as set by him through his dream and vision for his future. It is only on accomplishment that he is classified as an achiever. Perhaps, he himself may not be certain about his final achievement but he maintains in himself his strong belief, confidence and firm determination throughout and never deviates from the path of his vision and dream despite hardships and difficulties. Thus, you have to look on these achievers with a benevolent and thoughtful viewpoint and admire their struggle and success story as fighters in real life against heavy odds and adversities.

Odds and Adversities

By and large, most of the achievers are born in adverse conditions of some nature. Some of them inherit these conditions right from the day of their birth or childhood or later the adulthood. The time when the adversities occur is not known and they may happen anytime and anywhere in their life. Let us take a look at the types of adversities which are listed below:

a) Birth in extreme poverty.
b) Birth in the most backward area, region where no transport, education facilities are available.
c) Birth in rural areas where schooling facilities and connectivity are poor.
d) Birth with a physical handicap.
e) Birth at inhospitable places where extreme climatic conditions exist.
f) Loss of leg or hand movements due to polio or any other serious ailment in childhood.
g) Loss of parental umbrella and care in early childhood.
h) Loss of father or mother or both in an accident at early adulthood.
i) Upbringing under unsocial, unhygienic and uncultured environment.
j) Upbringing by the parents especially father who happens to have bad habits like drinking, gambling, etc.
k) Loss of body features in accident or natural calamities or war bombing.

There are innumerable ways in which the misfortunes may befall on an individual irrespective of the gender, caste, creed and religion as it makes no discrimination whenever it occurs. Misfortunes know no barriers and no boundaries and strike without any warning. It leaves you aghast and frightened with worries about your present and future.

Handicap Level and Trading Off

Any of these misfortunes causes a setback and creates a handicap in their life to rise from the present level which happens to be fairly low. The persons who do not face such misfortunes remain miles ahead of those who happen to bear the handicaps. Thus, these children or persons start their life with a basic handicap level of varying dimensions. So, they have firstly to face the challenge to overcome this handicap level, rise and come up to the level field at par with other fortunate children or persons.

Incidentally, this handicap level becomes the biggest obstacle and challenge to face and overcome. Those who cross and rise like a Phoenix bird are definitely poised to become an Achiever. In fact, such persons or children have to pass through a series of obstacles and demonstrate their mental strength, caliber, potential and talent at every important stage of life like school and college final year examinations, sports, debating competition and other academic activities. Whenever they excel and achieve top grading in such activities, they receive public attention and deserve its patronage and support for their meritorious performance and encourage them for further progress and higher achievements.

Role of Introspection

Now for those with a handicap as described above, they need not worry. The first and foremost need of the day is for them to strongly believe in the Will and Blessing of the God. They should strongly and firmly believe that they have been endowed with a gift in some other form with which they should try to overcome their handicap. This firm and strong belief in the God's impartiality, justice and unbiased dispensation enables you to look within yourself and search for that gift or power that is the compensation for the handicap from your birth or later. Consequently, you have to take recourse to Introspection and search deep inside yourself for finding out your own treasure of specific positive qualities which the God had bestowed on you at the time of your birth in the form of a heavenly gift. It is now you who have to search and discover through the process of introspection and self-assessment.

What is most important at this stage is your firm belief in the divine power which is an integral part of your inner Self. It leaves its imprint on your personality, attitude, mindset, aptitude, talent and interest areas. It becomes evident in the form of some of your body features like nose, eyes or forehead. So, for discovering the treasure of your positive attributes, you have to adopt the self-addressed process of:

a) **Introspection**

b) **Self-Assessment**

c) **Self-Appraisal**

d) **Self-Interrogation**

Once, you adopt the above self-centric processes honestly and sincerely, you get the answers which amazingly awaken you about your real potential, power, talent and abilities. You come to know about your weak points and realise their adverse effects on your relations and performance. You should naturally try to control and mitigate them as much as possible so that you don't suffer from their adverse effects. Once you gain control on your weak points, you should concentrate on strong points of your nature, character and behaviour. In fact, you should draw a balance sheet of your strong and weak points from the exercise of self-assessment. Consequently, you get a very vivid realistic picture of yourself. It is now up to you where to emphasize and where to control so that you are able to fully harness your abilities, potential and power for achievement of your cherished objectives in life.

Words of Wisdom – Guidelines

For becoming an achiever, you have to pragmatically accept certain facts of life, nature and supreme control of the divine power. You have to accept that the nature follows certain rules and regulations and it never crosses the limit as for example the ocean, wind, earth and so on. Whenever they do so, they cause havoc but after letting off their outburst, they come back to the normal state. So, they stay within their limits. They follow certain rules and go through certain periodic cycles. The consequent changes and transformations are the two processes which are dynamic and cyclic in nature. What are those imperceptible unwritten rules and words of wisdom? Let us take a look at them.

a) **Life is a series of changes.** It has to go through many seasons of dryness, hardships as well as pleasantness, warmth and joy and they don't last long.

b) **See the dream and have a vision.** That inspires as you go through the adversity. That enables you to remain focused on your goal and directs you to navigate in the specific direction with all your might, strength and power.

c) **Personal growth from sufferings.** Sufferings always lay foundation for you to become strong, bold and courageous. It awakens your spirit and kindles a fire for rising upwards.

d) **Failure is the seed of your future success.** Failure is a temporary phase and it carries the seed for your future successful period to come. Remember that nothing is permanent. Take your failure with a pinch of salt and regain your energies and spirit to strike back with might and vigor.

e) **Keep mental balance during the tough times.** As you encounter adverse and tough situations, you should maintain calm, discipline and routine schedule of your life. You should keep four dimensions of yourself in operating order and balanced condition i.e. the mind, body, emotions and spirit.

f) **Forget the past and think of the present and future.** Don't waste your precious time in discussing the past events. Learn from the mistakes you committed and honestly own up them. It enables you to conserve energy and concentrate on performance of the day with an eye on planning for the future.

g) **Always remember that you are not alone.** You are passing up the stream along with others. You are never alone. The spirit of being together creates warmth and confidence and negates isolation.

These are the hard truths or facts of human life one must know and remember with the knowledge and wisdom at the back of your mind. You are always inspired, encouraged and motivated to do something different from others, something beyond your handicaps and something beyond your present state. These words of wisdom enliven your spirit and morale for continuing your struggle. Once, your hidden spirit is awakened, you are poised for rapid strides on the correct path. No adversity, shortcomings or sufferings can then stop you.

Positive Attributes of an Achiever

Having words of wisdom and guidelines as stated above which constitute the foundation for facing the hardships, you get a broad vision which expands and enhances beyond the conventional boundaries. That vision enlightens the spirit and fire within you and brings out the following positive attributes of great importance to the forefront:

a) Intensive willpower and firm determination for achievement.

b) Clarity in vision and commitment to specific purpose.
c) Extreme devotion and dedication.
d) Concentration of efforts and involvement with focus on the objective.
e) High responsiveness and adaptability.
f) Creative and productive approach and attitude.
g) Self-control and self-correction.
h) Endurance and tolerance.
i) Tremendous self-confidence.
j) Objectivity and clarity in communication skills.
k) Human, gentle, polite and amiable relationship.
l) Intensive desire for learning and self-advancement.

These are highly important and distinct personal positive attributes of an achiever. They start demonstrating their influence on his personality and performance. Once a handicapped person decides and firms up his mind and vision, his hidden treasure of the positive attributes is invoked and activated. Once they start operating, thereafter nothing can stop him from his journey towards his destination.

In this respect, it is pointed out that the positive attributes as stated above are invariably present in the people but in different proportions, forms and varying strengths. Where their quantitative proportions are low, the performance of such individuals is average or below average and you do not find any substantive improvement in them. As the strengths and quantitative levels of these positive attributes increase, they correspondingly start demonstrating their influence in the positive manner. Now, it is generally observed that the handicapped persons possess these attributes in high order because they have to be stronger since half of their strength is consumed in overcoming their initial handicap levels and establish level playing field with others. Initial struggle and traditional framework of their minds need a lot of positive energy in order to lift them up from their base levels. Once they are up, there is nothing to stop them as they master the art and technique of advancement. Consequently, they start conducting themselves in highly responsible, committed and dedicated manner. Their strong will power, firm determination and commitment to their vision are quite evident and complimentary. They would like to stand on their own footing and proceed with a strong attitude and positive approach which drives and motivates them to compete with others and excel in performance. It is this spirit, urge, attitude and moral strength that drives them towards their objectives with fire in their inner Self to do better in their selected fields. Examples of such people who have really become achievers are numerous, like Sudha Chandran, Ravindra Jain, Helen Keller, war-injured soldiers and so on.

Extra Factor

It is also known as **Plus Factor**. It is really interesting to know about our Self that there is intense power and potential which stay hidden within us. If they are properly and judiciously tapped, they can remarkably change the course of our life. This power and potential are invisible, imperceptible and intangible but completely real and can certainly be harnessed. Our life can dramatically be transformed under their influence with proper guidance. They create strong life force and spirit after activation so that they drive a person to cope up with ever increasing complexities of the modern living and boldly face its challenges. We are basically concerned with the special concentration of the above stated positive attributes which consequently form a strong formidable life force that is generally known as Extra Factor or Plus Factor of our Self. What it means is that each positive attribute carries extra energy, extra potential, extra enthusiasm and extra eagerness. It is this extra energy associated with certain important positive attributes and when harnessed by certain persons that makes them different, special, remarkable and prominent in the public life and society. It requires deep insight into their personalities and inner Self for activating these latent forces. This extra factor is responsible for enabling a person to realise his dream. As a result, his existence and conduct become remarkably significant, bearable and recognisable.

It is generally observed that you are normally working much below your real potential and latent power. In fact, you are not aware about them or their depth and never try to know about them. With this indifferent attitude, you don't remain aware about your creative potential, problem solving capabilities and productive energies that are locked inside you and remain hidden, unaddressed and inactive. It is only your distinct dream, intense desire, willpower and farsighted vision that lay the seed for rising and upliftment. It leads to activate and release your latent power and potential. Here, your intense desire to pursue your creative dream tenaciously drives you towards your goal with the firm belief in the God to help and grant you enough strength and courage to face and overcome problems and difficulties and finally lead you to success. In a way, your sincere and honest worship, prayer and firm belief in the God inspire and encourage you to work hard with unshakable determination and strong will power for accomplishing your objectives and reaching your final destination.

Ultimately, you have to keep your plus factor active and maintain its momentum by injecting into your thought process, thought pattern and life style a few golden principles and values which arise by virtue of possessing certain important positive attributes such as faith, positive thinking, affirmative attitude, commitment, firmness in determination, communicative skills, humbleness and fairness in relations. It should be noted that when you have such an approach, attitude with positive mindset and clear distant vision, you certainly grow bigger in your own eyes. You feel mature and broad minded and you get a positive vision to look at the human life. As a result, you feel fire and upsurge within you. Consequently, you are driven and motivated at every stage to spontaneously work hard and maintain momentum and dynamism of the life force. In the process, your mental attitude, strain and complex feeling are reduced and you start feeling relief, happiness, peace of mind and relaxation even in the tense competitive environment. In fact, you learn the technique of laughing at the odd and unpleasant things and display a smile and cheerfulness on your face despite your continuous struggle and fight.

The Role of Talent

Well, the need of possessing talent can't be overlooked and ignored. Talent is the basic intelligence which covers average intellect and abilities for organising, administering and managing events in personal life, office, community and public domains. It should enable you to enjoy doing, thinking, learning and practicing about an event of your interest or whatever duties are assigned to you. In other words, it demonstrates your aptitude, urge, response and willingness to learn and capacity to think and act. In a way, it becomes indicator of your IQ (Intelligence Quotient) Level. When your IQ level is sufficiently high, it inspires and guides you to think, generate your thought process and decision making mechanism. You are activated to act, work and perform with specific purpose, dedication and interest. You don't act recklessly but apply your mind to think and then firmly decide. You don't hesitate, fumble and get confused. Your thinking is clear and your focus is on the objective. It should however be noted that you may have talent for application to positive purpose or negative purpose. Remember that talent does not mean high intellect or genius. It simply stands for your intellectual activism which may be for good purpose or bad purpose. And it depends upon his or her mindset, traditions, attitude and environmental conditions.

By and large, you must have observed that a handicapped person is highly intelligent and displays his talent in his expression, work style, hobbies, body language and certain gestures. His expressions are remarkably clear, sharp and impressive. I have seen a handicapped boy who was crippled and bound to wheel chair. He made jokes and people profusely laughed at them. His voice and expression were sharp, his sound was clear, high pitched and vibrant. He produced jokes and laughter with his sharp observation and pointed expression. Thus, he made a name for himself as an artist.

Positive Aspects of an Achiever

It is observed that a person who is an achiever loves his job, enjoys his performance, dedicates himself to the cause and aims at becoming the top performer. In the process, he becomes a positive thinker who never allows his mind to wander and catch negatives. He believes in the divine power and regularly prays before God. He pursues learning new things and develops his professional skills and uptake. He maintains quality and high standards in work, conduct and relations. He does not waste his time in gossiping and petty politics. He stays away from bad company. He is selective about his friend circle. He maintains contact and friendship with a selected lot. He moves forward towards his goals with confidence and commitment. He seeks advice and patronage from the competent persons and he never hesitates or feels any complex in doing so. Definitely, a person of this type is poised to become an excellent performer with self-esteem and self-pride.

Introspection – The Key Factor

Introspection remains the key factor as the main technique to find out what you possess in the realm of positive and negative domains. The moment you want to be an achiever in life and why not, you should spare a little time to study your personality and take a deep insight within yourself. Introspection enables to appraise you about your values, position, talent, worthiness and potential. It is a process of gaining control of yourself and start looking for possession of the treasure of your qualities which may have high contents of either positive or negative types. You are in a position to draw a balance sheet of positive and negative qualities and weigh the chances of becoming a good performer and in turn an achiever of your cherished dream and vision. With a little advice, guidance and motivation, you are able to get a true, realistic picture of your power, potential, strength and prospects. Once the picture is affirmative and commensurate with your dream and strong vision, you put yourself in top gear and drive the engine of your career with full speed. Of course, you should be cautious, mentally alert and responsive to external environment. You should often seek proper advice whenever in trouble, maintain positive attitude and face the risks and challenges with courage and boldness. You should always maintain fire and urge within yourself and that will surely drive and motivate you towards your objective.

Thus, you will finally observe that Introspection lays a scientific foundation to enable you to advance towards your objective in a logical, rational and purposeful manner. It reveals your direct responsibility, involvement and accountability in your lifelong functions and activities. So, it plays a very important role and becomes a key factor for achieving success or reducing eventual losses from failure in your service career.

Epilogue

It is strongly felt that this book and its contents are adequate enough to offer effective guidance and definite direction to those persons who wish to select the right path and seek right advice for self-improvement and enrichment of their career. Introspection and self-assessment are positive and constructive steps and offer correct and proper solution to the confused state of their mind. In this process, you get a clear picture of your inner Self where you observe good and bad as well as strong and weak points of your personality in a self-addressed introspective mode. In fact, you get a realistic projection of yourself for carrying out real assessment and appraisal of your nature, character, potential, abilities, habits and performance. Thus, you avail a unique opportunity to know where you stand and how much efforts and struggle you will have to really make for achieving your lifetime objectives.

You are expected to be honest, sincere, truthful, frank and conscious in your mind while adopting the exercise and process of Introspection and self-assessment. Since the direct method is advocated in this book, it becomes your self- addressed exercise. Obviously, it offers you realistic information about yourself in the form of your qualities of both positive and negative types. Achievement of your end objectives are finally determined by your personal attributes or qualities. What you ultimately achieve in life in the form of success or failure invariably occurs in direct proportion to what type of mix of positive and negative qualities and their synergetic proportional levels you possess and how you utilise them. You have also seen direct correlation of your destiny with your personal qualities in the form of a step-by-step approach in Chapter 7 with a large number of intermediate interactive unseen stages, each causing its influence on the next one thereby making your personal qualities and destiny as two interdependent entities.

As a matter of fact, the word destiny now becomes more meaningful and expressive about your action and deeds and the results you directly get thereof. By observing this correlation between the mystic aspects of your destiny and your personal attributes, it is strongly believed that you receive your personal qualities as a gift which is endowed to you at the time of your birth by the heavenly and earthly forces. You in fact carry them as an imprint of your destiny from the combination of some cosmic forces as existing at the time of your birth and some forces genetically passed on to you from your parents. Consequently, your nature, character, behaviour, talent, abilities, mindset and personality are influenced by your personal attributes and in turn your success and failure to which you call destiny.

It should be remembered that time which is linked with right opportunities is the essence of your life and waits for no one. It is your star and star plus qualities which drive and motivate you to make the best use of time and opportunities whenever they come your way. Those who utilise them with a sense of sincerity, involvement and commitment succeed in seeking wealth, fortune, fame, position and prosperity in life. Those who miss them eventually fail or lose. Consequently, they keep cursing their destiny which they find as the best alibi to explain their failure or loss which has in fact occurred due to the influence of some of the dominating negative attributes.

It is seen that many persons get promotions and reach senior positions of ranks, some of them get further promotions and reach higher ranks of status and a few of them really reach the top slots in their service career. They are called very lucky or fortunate persons. Unfortunately, some critics may look on their achievements as gains through favour or by adopting unscrupulous means. Thus, they try to grossly underestimate and undervalue their achievements by uncharitable remarks without realising the important and domineering role played by their star and star plus qualities in their success at every step in their service career and that too in a highly competitive environment. In so doing, they do the worst type of disservice to themselves thereby leaving no scope for self-correction and improvement and continue to stay in their world of false self-pride and esteem.

Hence, you should remain fair, honest and truthful to yourself and admit your deficiencies and weaknesses on account of possessing certain dominating negative attributes which eventually cause and lead to failure or loss in your life. Such type of approach enables you to avail a chance for self-improvement and remain aware and conscious to avoid loss or failure partially if not fully at a later date in life.

Having considered personal attributes as human endowments given at the time of birth, there is always scope for self-development through influence, caused by parental care, education and upbringing, environment and yoga / meditation. The degree of their influence is however determined by the responsive, assimilative, proactive and mission oriented mind of the recipient. In other words, attributes like responsiveness, adaptability, drive, initiative and will power with mission oriented approach will determine the effect of these external factors and agencies on you. The degree of presence of these attributes in human beings varies quite considerably and bears direct correlation to the relative strength and dominance of either positive or negative attributes. This ultimately determines the end result of success or failure in the life mission of an individual. dominance of positive attributes causes positive influence of these external agencies and further gets enhanced by adopting self-development measures according to its road map as given in Chapter 4 of this book. Steps as suggested in this road map of self-development are practical and based on personal experience of the author during his long service period in the Army and Industry.

A candidate has to appear for an interview and participate in meetings and group discussions. His three main traits such as personality, aptitude and motivation which broadly cover the entire attribute profile are critically observed and assessed by the Board members in order to ascertain his suitability for a particular job / service during the limited time available to them. Constraints factors of an interview are stated in order to appraise a candidate for getting correct picture and scenario of the interview and its environment. Candidates generally overlook the visible important factors of their personality and walk in for the interview without careful preparation and taking proper steps for improving their personality and appearance. Positive and practical steps and guidelines are given in order to improve your personality before you face the interview board.

In order to summarise the objective of this book, a set of five pertinent and prominent questions which are intended with a view point for ascertaining your profile of abilities and potential are given at the end of Chapter 4 of this book.

Concept of success and failure are clarified with a view to take some lessons from past events and draw useful conclusions. In fact, failure and especially when it occurs at the very initial stage becomes very painful and discouraging. At this stage, a sympathetic and optimistic approach is strongly advisable for adoption along some positive and constructive guidance and consolation to such candidates.

Having come to know about your attributes and their correlation with success or failure, you are in a position to write your own Personal Performance Report (PPR) perhaps in the same manner as your superior officer annually writes on you and your performance. From this report, you may realise the expectations of your employer and how you are able to partially or fully meet them. You also get a positive clue that you alone are the sole controller and arbitrator of your destiny which no longer remains mystic for materialising your career objectives. In this respect, introspection and self-assessment reveal your direct responsibility, involvement and accountability in your activities and deeds. As a result, they play a very important role in unfolding the secrets of your career oriented destiny.

A format for preparing your Self-Assessment and Self-Appraisal Report is enclosed as Annexure 2 to Chapter 3. It gives you ready references and also brings out certain prominent features of your nature in the form of answers to certain introspective questions. It acts as a guide and enables you to adopt a Self-Development Programme and take timely corrective measures against your weaknesses and negative features.

Besides making a career for your financial living, you can make it exciting and prosperous to bring you happiness and peace. Any career / job has to be a productive activity. You no doubt need financial security from your career but you should also expect other benefits outside this scope. In fact, your life involves around four areas of activities such as paid work, home work, gift/ charity work and study work. In short, fulfilment comes from a varied life and not from monotonous way of life. You should give enough time for creativity, reflection, meditation and to relations such as with your family members and friends. Effective time management can help you here. At any time, you should harness your positive attributes for your self-development and bring your life under your own control thereby making it proactive, positive and assertive. Remember that your career should be for the right cause for making your life active, prosperous and exciting rather than dying, rich, lonely and unsatisfied.

Finally, this book offers you a practical and powerful guide to awaken you to realise that you remain at the center stage of your lifetime activities. Consequently, you become the Architect of your career and eventually your career oriented destiny. It is also pointed out that Introspection and self-assessment play a highly important role in enabling you to become an achiever against heavy odds and adversities. So, you should always set aside time for yourself to do introspection and carry-out self-assessment honestly and sincerely. It will definitely pay rich dividends in helping you to effectively managing and advancing your career and boldly facing the challenges of the twenty-first century.

Direct Technique for Self-Assessment: A Comprehensive List of Positive and Negative Attributes Phase One

Comprehensive List

Examine the list, think over, understand fully and then under Yes/No, tick if you possess that negative attribute. Mark X if you do not possess it.

List of Positive Attributes

Sl.No.	*Types of Attributes*	*Description and meaning of attributes*	*CGS/ CPA*	*Yes/ No*
1.	Adaptable +	Flexibility in adjusting to a new or changing situation or people or job conditions.	CPA	
2.	Accommo-dative	Capacity to accept others view point and their choice and your readiness to accept.	CPA	
3	Assertive	To state views firmly or insist to be right.	CPU	
4	Confident	Trust about self.	CGS	
5	Consci-entious*	Careful and earnest in work and relationship.	CPA	
6	Creative/ Innovative	Urge to generate new ideas and produce work	CPA	
7	Communicative+	Willing to pass information and get in touch to remain in contact.	CPA	

(Contd...)

(Contd...)

8	Cooperative*	Willing to work or act together.	CPA
9	Consistent	Not changing views or quality, remaining the same.	CPA
10	Dedicated*	Giving up oneself wholly to a cause or job or work.	CGS
11	Decisive+	Capacity to quickly arrive at logical conclusion and decide on a definite course of action.	CPA
12	Dependability*	Working constantly and independently without supervision and accepting additional obligations.	CGS
13	Driving and determined+	Firmness of mind and vigor in execution of tasks and ability to prevail upon others.	CGS
14	Endurance & stamina*	Physical and mental fitness and capacity to bear stress and strain for successful work under adverse conditions.	CGS
15	Enthusiastic	Acting with one's own power, interest and keenness.	CGS
16	Expressive*	Ability to express verbally and in writing.	CPA
17	Gentle and polite	Polite.	CGS
18	Honest*	Truthful. Not to steal or cheat or defraud.	CGS
19	Initiative+	Readiness to take first step or act of own without anybody directing to do so.	CGS
20	Ingenious	Skill of devising means and resources to solve unforeseen problems or meeting contingencies.	CPA

(Contd...)

(Contd...)

21	Hard working*	To try hard and put continuous efforts against difficulties.	CGS
22	Intelligent	Mental ability to grasp and understand quickly and cleverly.	CGS
23	Integrity+	Honest and just approach in personal and official dealings and relationship.	CPA
24	Leadership	Ability to lead and remain ahead in assigned tasks and jobs.	CPA
25	Logical	Reasoning correctly and as per the rules.	CPA
26	Loyal*	Willing and faithful in providing support in service to your superiors and subordinates.	CGS
27	Keen and eager*	Urge to learn and act of one's own.	CGS
28	Meticulous	Careful and accurate about even smaller details.	CGS
29	Memory	Power to remember and store information. Not to be forgetful.	CGS
30	Mature	Understanding and balance as per one's age and service.	CPA
31	Mission-oriented+	Aim to achieve end objective at any cost.	CPA
32	Morality*	Having to do with right and wrong behaviour and character.	CPA
33	Optimistic	Taking bright and hopeful view of events and situations.	CGS
34	Perseverent+	To keep trying to do a job in spite of problems and difficulties.	CGS

(Contd...)

(Contd...)

35 Persuasive	To bring a person around to do or think by arguing or advising him to your way or liking.	CPA
36 Persistent	To hold fast or remain firm in pursuit objectives in spite of difficulties.	CPA
37 Pragmatic	Concerned with the matter of fact, being practical instead of ideal or talking loosely without practical aspect.	CPA
38 Prudent	Wise and cautious	CPA
39 Reliable*	Being trustworthy, being faithful.	CGS
40 Responsible*	Moral feelings to own consequences.	CGS
41 Responsive+	Quick to show interest or react or answer to situation.	CGS
42 Sensible*	Having or showing wisdom or common sense, being functional.	CGS
43 Sensitive	Feeling mental pain about others or getting affected by small external changes.	CPA
44 Sincere*	Honest in words and deeds meaning what one says, it means true.	CGS
45 Sociable	Fond of company of friends, relations and others. Ability to get along others.	CPA
46 Sacrifice	Act of giving or offering something at own cost for good of others.	CPA
47 Studious	To gain knowledge by reading regularly, sincerely and carefully.	CPA
48 Talented	Special ability or skill.	CPA

(Contd...)

(Contd...)

49	Tactful	Dealing with people so as to avoid hurting or offending.	CPA
50	Tenacity+	Will to do or pursue well in face of odds and difficult situation.	CGS
51	Will power+	Mental power to choose, decide and act.	CGS
52	Willingness*	Ready to do and act what is asked or ordered for.	CGS
53	Vision+	Ability to see and envisage the future events.	CGS
54	Updating and upgrading	Desire to improve and undergo training for self improvement.	CPA
55	Ambition+	Desire for success, power, fame aimed as goal in life.	CGS
56	Awareness*	Having some prior knowledge or being conscious implying mental alertness.	CGS
57	Intuition	Power of grasping a fact or idea without thinking it out.	CPA

Legend

CGS—Stands for Career Guidance & Selection.

CPA—Stands for Career Promotion & Advancement

Attributes are classified under two specific applications under legends CGS and CPA. It should be noted that attributes under CPA are needed in addition to attributes under CGS for those persons who are already in service and essentially for the promotional purpose. Attributes under CGS are essentially needed for any career / service for ever. Attributes with star (*) mark are essential and with plus (+) are desirable / optional or specific to a particular service like Defence.

List of Negative Attributes

Sl.No.	*Types of Attributes*	*Description and meaning of attributes*	*Yes or No*	*Remarks*
1.	Angry*	Losing temper or feeling bitter or getting into rage.		
2	Adamant*	Unwilling to give way or sticking to own views.		
3	Aggressive	Ability to push one's interest forcefully. Self-assertive in offensive manner.		
4	Ambiguous	Lacking clarity in views and opinion, having vague ideas.		
5	Ambusive	Using indecent language or expression.		
6	Careless	Paying little attention.		
7	Crazy	Over enthusiastic, showing some stupidity.		
8	Disorderly	Lacking neatness or orderliness. Untidy.		
9	Demanding	Habit of considering own interest. Insistent.		
10	Domineering*	Feeling arrogantly that one is too sure and right and dominant		
11	Egoistic	Talking much high or boasting of oneself.		
12	Emotional*	Moving the feelings that excite the mind quickly & easily. Liable to emotions.		
13	Envious*	Discontented due to what others have like wealth, fame, promotion.		
14	Flamboyant	Show off with the intention to attract notice or attention.		
15	Greedy	Selfish desire or interest to possess. Selfishly desirous.		
16	Hypocrite	Pretend to be good or false show of goodness.		

(Contd...)

(Contd...)

17	Immoral	Indecent. Behaviour not according to ethics, manner or principles.
18	Impulsive*	Urge or feeling, resulting in sudden action without thinking.
19	Indifferent	Showing no interest of good or bad.
20	Introvert*	Looking inward and remaining confined to yourself.
21	Indecent*	Offending against normal or usual standards of behaviour.
22	Malicious	Carrying ill will or bad feeling about others.
23	Nervous*	Getting easily excited or frightened on seeing challenges or unpleasant events.
24	Obstinat	Stubborn, not yielding to rational arguments.
25	Overriding	Setting aside or ignoring rules or authority. Claiming superiority over others.
26	Overstepping	To go beyond the limit or rule or boundary.
27	Passive	Offering no resistance or opposition or showing no reaction.
28	Passionate*	Feeling strongly or getting easily moved on anger or love matters. Dominated by strong feelings.
29	Pugnacious	Fond of fighting or quarreling.
30	Rigid*	Holding views or behaviour which is stiff and not bending or yielding.
31	Rude*	Showing bad manners or impolite behaviour.
32	Selfish	Caring only for self pleasure or advantage or interest.

(Contd...)

(Contd...)

33	Servile	Behaving like a slave or showing lack of self respect.
34	Short-sighted*	Lacking imagination or foresight. Not thinking of the future.
35	Stubborn*	Unwilling to give way or difficult to manage or deal with.
36	Self-centered	Concerned with own affairs or interests.
37	Sulky	Keeping silent because one dislikes things against own wish. Resentfully silent.
38	Tempera-mental*	Becoming excited or having emotional nature while reacting to the situation.

(In the column under Yes / No, tick if you possess that negative attribute. Mark X if you do not possess it.)

Note

Marking of the symbol star (*) against a particular attribute indicates its relatively high damaging nature from behavioral point of view in any career / service. As such, these attributes from this negative List are pointed out as negative star qualities and must be kept under control in order to avoid their adverse effects on your performance and conduct.

Phase Two

Having examined and ticked your attributes in the first phase, think over to what extent and proportion you possess those attributes and then proceed to quantify them in terms of various grades/ranks/marks as shown in the following table.

Positive Attributes

(Positive Ranking / Grading)

Sl.No.	*Types of attributes for ranking (How much)*	*Yes/ No*	*Ext (+9) No*	*Vg (+7)*	*Ave (+5)*	*Low (+3)*	*None (o)*
1.	Adaptable+						
2	Assertive						
3	Ambitious*						
4	Aware*						
5	Confident*						
6	Conscientious*						
7	Creative/ Innovative						
8	Communicative+						
9	Cooperative*						
10	Consistent						
11	Dedicated*						
12	Decisive+						
13	Dependable*						
14	Driving and determined+						
15	Endurance and stamina*						
16	Enthusiastic						
17	Expressive+						
18	Gentle and polite*						
19	Honest*						
20	Initiative+						

21 Ingenious
22 Intuition
23 Intelligent
24 Integrity+
25 Hard work * and struggle
26 Leadership+
27 Logical
28 Loyal*
29 Keenness*
30 Meticulous
31 Memory
32 Mature
33 Mission-oriented +
34 Morality*
35 Optimistic
36 Perseverent+
37 Persuasive+
38 Persistent+
39 Pragmatic
40 Prudent
41 Reliable*
42 Responsible*
43 Responsive+
44 Sacrifice
45 Sensible*
46 Sensitiv
47 Sincere*
48 Sociable
49 Studious+
50 Talented
51 Tactful
52 Tenacious+

53	Will power+
54	Willingness*
55	Vision +
56	Updating and upgrading
57	Accomodative

Legend

Ext—Excellent, Vg— Very good, Ave— Average.

Negative Attributes
(Negative Ranking/Marking)

Sl.No.	Types of attributes for ranking (How much)	Yes/ No	Ranking ALWS (-9)	VO (-7)	Ave (-5)	Sldm (-3)	Nil (0)
1.	Angry*						
2	Adamant*						
3	Aggressive						
4	Ambiguous						
5	Ambusive						
6	Careless						
7	Crazy						
8	Disorderly						
9	Demanding						
10	Domineering*						
11	Egoistic						
12	Emotional*						
13	Envious*						
14	Flamboyant						
15	Greedy						
16	Hypocrite						
17	Immoral						
18	Impulsive*						
19	indifferent						
20	Indecent*						
21	Malicious						
22	Nervous*						
23	Obstinate						
24	Overstepping						
25	Introvert*						
26	Overriding						
27	Passive						
28	Passionate*						

(Contd...)

(Contd...)

29	Pugnacious
30	Rigid*
31	Rude*
32	Selfish
33	Servile
34	Short-sighted*
35	Stubborn*
36	Self-centred
37	Sulky
38	Temperamental*

Legend

ALWS— Always or all the time or excessive, VO— Very often, Ave— Average or often Sldm—Seldom or sometimes.

Operating Instructions for Second Phase

Please study the following instructions before you start ticking and marking your score for possessing attributes of both types as stated above.

1. These instructions are applicable for marking both types of above stated attributes.
2. Self-explanation or meaning is briefly given against each attribute. You may refer to the dictionary for its clear and deep meaning if required, since full understanding is essential before you start marking your score.
3. Maximum marks allotted to each attribute are 10 and 9 out of 10 is considered as upper limit for full allotment of practical nature since 10 out 10 score is not possible.
4. Grading or scaling for allotment of marks to each attribute you possess should be done according to the following scale.

For positive attributes

— Assign Positive (+) marks as under

— Excellent. +9, Very Good. +7, Good or Average or Medium. +5, Low or Below Average. +3, Nil or None. 0

For negative attributes

-— Assign Negative (—) marks as under-

— Always or All the time. - 9, Very Often. - 7, Often or Average or Medium. -5, Sometimes or seldom. - 3, Nil or None. 0

6. The above marking is done as per the grade you assess about yourself and should be stated in the last column marked against each attribute after understanding it fully.

SUPPLEMENT TO ANNEXURE 1 OF CHAPTER 2 (CONTINUED)

Assessment of Talent in the form of Abilities

Indicatation of abilities for performing various tasks/functions/ duties/assignments/projects while you are in service, business or of your own in personal life.

This is another way of assessing your attributes by asking you to take a look at your abilities for performance.

Examine, study, think over and then mark/rank each of your abilites on one to ten scale as before.

Firstly, tick if you possess. Mark 'X' if you do not possess.

Sl.No.	*Abilities to*	*Yes/ No*	*Ran (9)*	*(7)*	*(5)*	*(3)*	*(0)*
1.	Adapt to any change						
2.	Be accommodative to other's views						
3.	Cooperate & coordinate						
4.	Create & innovate						
5.	Communicate clearly your view						
6.	Analyse and select						
7.	Control temper						
8.	Drive and motivate						
9.	Discuss and negotiate						
10.	Bring up, nurture and train						
11.	Express verbally and in writing						
12.	Concentrate and focus attention						
13.	Keen and enthusiastic						
14.	Bear hardships and face challenges						
15.	Persistent and persuasive						
16.	Firm and decisive						
17.	Plan and execute						
18.	Perceive opportunities and avail						
19.	Strong and assertive						
20.	Tender and kind hearted						
21.	Generous and supporting						
22.	Dignified and self-esteemed						

23. Restrain emotions and temperament
24. Perceive and foresee
25. Form team and work together
26. Help and sacrifice
27. Grasp and assimilate
28. Study and work hard
29. Set mission and work for it
30. Lead a team/group/section/division
31. Listen and be patient
32. Dominate and demand
33. Be impulsive and emotional
34. Be social and mix with
35. Organise and manage
36. Be responsive and attentive
37. Have vision for planning
38. Work independently without supervision
39. Be rigid and rude
40. Be decent and soft-spoken
41. Be tactful and diplomatic in behaviour
42. Talk and discuss with smile on face
43. Be optimistic for bright future
44. Tolerate mistakes and omissions
45. Give presentation about your plans/ mission/project
46. Supervise work of your subordinates
47. Optimise use of money and manpower
48. Argue with logic and reason.

Self-Assessment and Self-Appraisal Report Form

1. Name.
2. Date of Birth.
3. Place of Birth and Type of Environment.
4. Academic Qualifications. (State Board and University level)
   a) Examination Passed
   b) Division/Grade First/Second/Third.
   c) Percentage of Marks.
   d) Distinction in Subjects if any.
5. Professional Qualifications
   a) Type of Course
   b) Degree Achieved
   c) Division/Grade First/Second/Third
   d) Percentage of Marks
6. Professional Courses/Training done if any
7. Details of Positive Attributes

   Identify Your Positive Attributes from the Comprehensive List as given in the Annexure 1 of Chapter 2 of this book and state under the heads of Star and Star Plus categories.
8. Details of Your Negative Attributes

   Identify Your Negative Attributes from the same list as applicable to you and highlight those which are Star Negative Type.

9. Self-Appraisal—SWAIT Analysis
   a) S—State strong points of your Nature and Personality
   b) W—State weak points of your Nature and Personality.
   c) A—Your Aptitude
   d) I——Your Interest Areas for Career/Course/Service.
   e) T—Threats to Yourself like your Age factor, Apprehension, Likes, Dislikes, Financial Bottlenecks, Competition

10. Intelligence Quotient (I.Q.)
    a) Very High
    b) High
    c) Moderate/Medium
    d) Low
    e) Very Low

11. Mindset—Mental Thinking , Approach and Viewpoints
    a) Positive or Negative
    b) Optimistic or Pessimistic
    c) Encouraging or Discouraging

12. Strictly Personal
    a) Drive and Motivation
    b) Will Power and Determination
    c) Loyalty and Commitment
    d) Responsive and Active
    e) Initiative and Awareness

13. Your Vision/Objectives/Ambition Level
    a) Very High - Reaching top level
    b) High — Reaching high levels
    c) Middle — Reaching senior level
    d) Supervisory Reaching section level
    e) Working - Remain as it is

14. Your Aspirations (What you wish to become or achieve)
    a) Fortune, Wealth, Money and Prosperity
    b) Power, Authority or Ruling
    c) Fame, Recognition, Awards
    d) Social and Public Service
    e) Self Business, Enterprise, Service or Entrepreneur
    f) Marketing, Sales or Business Promotion
    g) Religious and Spiritual Pursuits and Upliftment

15. Performance With
    a) Dedication, Responsibility and Commitment
    b) Quality Consciousness and Awareness
    c) Timely Completion and Reporting
    d) Updating of Professional Knowledge and Learning
    e) Aspiration to promotions of High ranks and Status
    f) Control on Self, Ego, Pride, Temperament and Habits
    g) Readiness for Shouldering Additional Responsibilities/Tasks

16. Temperament (State high, medium or low)
    a) Anger
    b) Sensitive and Emotional
    c) Critical, Sarcastic or Abusive
    d) Casual and Indifferent
    e) Egoistic and Self-praising
    f) Evasive and Shirking
    g) Calm and Composed
    h) Passionate

17. Family Background
    a) Rich/Middle/Average/Poor
    b) Educated or Uneducated
    c) Political, Social or Religious

d) Forward Looking or Unorthodox

e) Progressive or Conservative Viewpoint

f) Inspiring, Retarding or Regressive

g) Strongly/Highly/Moderately/Poorly Financially Supportive

h) Relatives — Encouraging or Discouraging

18. Academic Performance in Last Three Annual Examinations and Grade Achieved

a) Excellent (Above 91 %)

b) Very Good (Between 81 and 90 %)

c) Good (Between 61 and 80 %)

d) Average (Between 41 and 60 %)

e) Poor (Below 40 %)

19. Confidence Level (After considering above Factors)

f) Very High

g) High

h) Cautious

i) Needs Preparation

j) Average

k) Low

20. Health

l) Healthy

m) Strong and Tenacious

n) Stamina and Capacity for Hard Work and Tolerance

o) Physical Fitness

p) Endurance

Besides, some additional introspective questions are addressed to you as under:

1. How much time do you give to yourself to think about yourself, your activities and actual performance?

2. Have you ever truly assessed your potential, capabilities, talent, communicative skills, behavior and performance and ascertained their levels by asking how much?
3. How do you find your personal behavior, conduct, manners and relations with your family members, friends, relatives, colleagues, subordinates and senior officials? Is it amiable, cordial, friendly, gentle, polite or stiff, rough, stubborn, rigid, indifferent?
4. Have you ever thought of your aptitude and specific interest areas while selecting a particular career or job? Have you given them any importance?
5. What is your mindset? Is it positive or negative, constructive or destructive, forward or retrograde, appreciative or critical, progressive or regressive, pragmatic or conservative? Are you critical, indifferent, sarcastic or appreciative, admiring, encouraging towards works done by others?
6. Have you ever thought of the personal strengths and weaknesses in your nature, character, personality, behaviour? Did you try to exploit your strong points and control weak points?
7. Do you think too much of the past events and overlook the present and future?
8. How do you take the failure in life? Is it boldly, in right stride and spirit? What is your approach? Is it desperate, crestfallen, frightened or proactive, courageous, challenging with a great deal of optimism, hope and positive notion?
9. Do you want to do your self-development and self-Improvement? Have you any road map for achieving it?
10. Do you believe in your destiny? Where does it lie? Is it in your hands or personal qualities/attributes or elsewhere?

It is pointed out that if such a careful and meticulous report is prepared, it becomes a comprehensive record of your present status and sets the direction and momentum of your career. It enables you to take proper and right decision which is based on your personal status, abilities and potential. In fact, such Self-Assessment and Self-Appraisal Reports set a benchmark for effectively giving you guidance, advice and counseling for pushing forward your career prospects.

Format of a Typical Consoling Letter Advocating Introspection after Occurrence of First Failure in Life

My Dear,

I am sorry to come to know that you have suffered a setback in your academic progress or have not been able to clear the hurdle of competitive examination. I note that this was your first attempt for appearing in a widely open competitive examination conducted by an Independent Body. I further note that this has happened at a time when you are making beginning of your career in life. It has now offered you an opportunity to pause, deliberate and honestly think about your strong and weak points. It is also time for you to seriously ponder as to what and where things have gone wrong and how.

Hence, the question is how this has occurred and why things have gone wrong and how to overcome the situation. There is no point in blaming anyone including outside agencies and outside factors. There is no point in blaming your destiny as it is too early and premature. Then, how to find out the reasons as unless you do that , you can not adopt remedial measures and take corrective action.

It is therefore right time to introspect and understand if you have committed some mistakes and made wrong judgment and took wrong decisions. If so, did it occur knowingly or unknowingly, consciously or subconsciously? What important points did you overlook? Were you systematic and methodical in your approach to studies? Were you over confident and over optimistic? Are there any negative factors that made you casual, indifferent or nervous?

So, it is right time for you to introspect and critically carry out a self-assessment. You should look deep within yourself and recollect if you have committed serious mistakes which you should now frankly and honestly admit. Think over if you lacked in your systematic studies, dedication and commitment to the cause you cherished. Remember that you have to firstly search your house and then only point out your finger at others. This is no doubt a bold, courageous and rational step you should adopt. It will certainly lead you to take timely corrective actions and help in your renewed preparation.

Please do not get disheartened by this opportunity loss. This has given you a chance to become more cautious, careful and wiser and become bold to face the challenges in life in a better manner. You should see the positive side of this incident provided you learn from your past mistakes and take corrective actions properly. A bright future will not be far off.

Please remember that any failure is never final and it is not the end of the world. But, it can be a positive beginning to enable you to achieve success in your subsequent attempts. You must therefore take your failure gracefully and coolly and act boldly with composed mind and try to maintain morale high with positive and optimistic outlook for your bright future. You should see the seed of your success in this failure and remember that it will not last long. You alone can make your career and achieve your ambition. What you must have is the will power, vision, confidence, drive, motivation and adaptability to pursue your intensive efforts for the mission, you have in your life.

In this context, I trust, the following quote of Michael Jordan, one of the most celebrated basket ball players of USA will prove inspiring to you.

"I have missed more than 9000 shots. I have lost almost 300 games. I have failed over and over again in my life. And that is why I succeeded."

Wishing you the very best in life,

Yours sincerely

Format of a Specimen Annual Confidential Report (ACR)

Headings used for Describing Various Attributes

Various attributes of an employee are covered under the following heads for describing their different functions and activities.

a) Entirely Personal Attributes, covering Nature, Character and Potential
b) Relation, covering Conduct and Behaviour
c) Educational and Professional Qualifications
d) Performance under Different Roles
e) Communication Skill
f) Challenges and Adventure
g) Leadership
h) Contribution and Achievements
i) Special Remarks especially on negative / weak points

Specimen of a Typical ACR

Your immediate superior officer who is called the Initiating Officer (IO) will report on you and your performance in a typical manner as under:

Entirely Personal Attributes

Extremely or highly honest, sincere, hard working and dedicated person; adaptable to any environment; highly mature, logical and dependable, meticulous and mission oriented in approach; carries high sense of responsibility, accountability and commitment; moderately intelligent but has tenacity and determination;

moderately temperamental; domineering in views and opinions; needs to control temper and avoid rigidity in approach.

Relationship

Highly social, cooperative, and attentive to needs of his or her subordinates; polite and humble while dealing with seniors; moderately soft and gentle in dealings.

Educational and Professional Qualifications

Highly qualified and possess professional knowledge commensurate to his technical qualifications and uses it meaningfully for the assigned jobs and responsibilities; takes deep interest in updating his knowledge and looks for attending training courses and workshops; displays practical approach with confidence.

Performance

Good in managing and organising activities; works with a strong sense of team spirit, comradeship and dedication; achieves assigned tasks with mission oriented zeal and spirit; has high communicative skill and respect for seniors as well as subordinates; practical, thoughtful, and judicious in utilising human and capital resources; owns responsibility and remains highly accountable to organisation; maintains high morale of his team and submit timely reports and feedback to superiors.

Leadership

Has strong will power, vision, determination and ambition; extremely loyal, dependable and resourceful; highly committed to the mission objectives and achieve result at all cost; encourage, motivates and trains his or her team; has command on expression and remains to the point; analytical and systematic in approach and planning.

Achievements

Participated in volleyball competition at state level and brought laurels to the organisation, suggested certain innovative procedures which resulted in economy of time and resources.

Special Remarks

Common words used generally to describe negative or weak points which should be selectively and carefully used in reporting are given as under:

– Domineering, Temperamental, Assertive, Introvert, Shuns public glare, needs control over temper and emotions, Aloof, Unsociable, Ambiguous, Biased, Reserved, Obsessed, Fastidious, Evasive, Conservative, Uninspiring, Obstructive, Slow & dull, Suspicious, Selfish, Envious, Impulsive, Indifferent, Servile, Self centered, Irrational, Sulky, Expensive, Extremely ambitious, Narrow minded.

Introspective Questions for Writing Personal Performance Report

It is pointed out that a report written by your superior officer in the typical format of Annual Confidential Report (ACR) may appear like the one as sample given above for illustration purpose. Since you are concerned with such a report, you are advised to adopt the technique of interrogating yourself and ascertain whether you are really performing your duties according to the expectations of your employer. Here, you should imagine yourself in your employer's place and think of those which you would have expected from your employee. So, you are advised to write a personal report by resorting to typical questioning to yourself about your conduct and performance as under:

1. Have you got loyalty and integrity towards your organisation?
2. Do you follow self discipline and code of conduct?
3. Are you hard working, diligent and industrious? Do you pursue your job with dedication, devotion and involvement?
4. Do you have adequate knowledge of your profession? Have you developed your professional skill and kept it updated?
5. Do you attend training programs and workshops willingly, regularly and attentively?
6. Have you got total sense of responsibility and commitment to your job?

7. Do you complete your assigned tasks within scheduled time? Do you like to be reminded for completion of your work?
8. Are you dependable and trustworthy? Do you submit correct reports and returns and own responsibility for any error, mistake or slip in reporting?
9. Do you work as a member of a team with the team spirit, cooperation and mutual support?
10. Are you gentle, amiable and polite in your behaviour?
11. Do you participate in petty politics and union activities?
12. Do you use your time, resources and manpower economically and optimally?
13. Do you participate in social activities and conduct social events?
14. Do you accept additional responsibilities willingly and volunteer for it?
15. Do you follow some values, principles and etiquettes in your work and business?
16. Are you a good listener? Do you interact while listening?
17. Can you express clearly, softly, gently and loudly in meetings, group discussion and presentation?
18. Do you appreciate the work of others and say a few words of appreciation?
19. Do you control your temperament on occurrence of any unpleasant event?
20. Do you get disappointed on occurrence of failure or take it boldly as a challenge to succeed?
21. Do you remain aware about the environment around you and activities which are taking place around?
22. Do you have the vision and foresight for tomorrow?

Answers to the above questions are sufficient for projecting your abilities, nature, character and relations. It is advisable to control and correct those areas of weaknesses and drawbacks and set them right in time. You also get a complete picture of yourself and now know where you stand with respect to your career prospects and achievement of prosperity.